The Inclusion Calculation

The Inclusion Calculation

Why Men Appropriate Women's Representation

MELODY E. VALDINI

OXFORD
UNIVERSITY PRESS

OXFORD
UNIVERSITY PRESS

Oxford University Press is a department of the University of Oxford. It furthers
the University's objective of excellence in research, scholarship, and education
by publishing worldwide. Oxford is a registered trade mark of Oxford University
Press in the UK and certain other countries.

Published in the United States of America by Oxford University Press
198 Madison Avenue, New York, NY 10016, United States of America.

Library of Congress Cataloging-in-Publication Data
Names: Valdini, Melody Ellis.
Title: The inclusion calculation : why men appropriate women's representation /
Melody Ellis Valdini.
Description: New York, NY : Oxford University Press, 2019. |
Includes bibliographical references and index.
Identifiers: LCCN 2019006327 (print) | LCCN 2019021433 (ebook) |
ISBN 9780190936211 (Updf) | ISBN 9780190936228 (Epub) |
ISBN 9780190936204 (paperback) | ISBN 9780190936198 (hardcover)
Subjects: LCSH: Women—Political activity. | Men—Political activity. |
Sex role—Political aspects. | Power (Social sciences)—United States. |
BISAC: POLITICAL SCIENCE / Political Process / Elections. |
POLITICAL SCIENCE / Political Process / General. | SOCIAL SCIENCE / Gender Studies.
Classification: LCC HQ1236 (ebook) | LCC HQ1236 .V346 2019 (print) |
DDC 320.082—dc23
LC record available at https://lccn.loc.gov/2019006327

9 8 7 6 5 4 3 2 1

Paperback printed by LSC Communication, United States of America
Hardback printed by Bridgeport National Bindery, Inc., United States of America

For my husband, who is the most beautiful dude in the world . . .
For my daughters, who are brilliant and fantastic in every way . . .
And for my sister, who is braver than me but doesn't realize it yet . . .
This book is dedicated to all of you, my sweet family.

CONTENTS

ACKNOWLEDGMENTS

I officially started writing this book on Mother's Day, 2015. Writing it was the gift that I was giving myself. Now that the babies were bigger, now that I had tenure, now that I could breathe, I finally got to write down the ideas that had been bouncing around my head for over a decade. It was a meaningful moment to start this book, and that meaningfulness continued throughout the project; writing this has meant the world to me, and I am so grateful to the many people who supported me on this journey.

I want to begin by recognizing my teachers because without them, I am certain this book (and my career in general) would not exist. They were instrumental in both growing my brain and being role models of kindness and generosity; there are no words that can express my gratitude for their help throughout the years. In particular, Mrs. Carolyn Loops, Mr. Ray Andrzejewski, Dr. Stephen Stambough, Dr. Shaun Bowler, and Dr. Matthew Shugart—thank you.

I could not have written this book without the librarians and resources of the Portland State University (PSU) library. Our library is alarmingly under-funded but fundamental to the mission of the university; I am grateful for the efforts of the librarians who make it work, even under duress. In particular, special thanks to Rick Mikulski for helping me hunt down the legislative transcripts of the Argentine Chamber of Deputies. In addition, the Reed College library generously (though perhaps unknowingly) provided me a quiet space to work for years, and the sweet and welcoming attitudes of their librarians, particularly Mark McDaniel, were instrumental to my productivity there. Thank you all so much. Libraries are the best.

I am deeply indebted to many people at PSU. First, thank you to Dean Stephen Percy of the College of Urban and Public Affairs for his continuing support of conference travel and research assistants, even during these lean budget times. I also want to recognize the support and encouragement of my colleagues in the political science department, particularly Chris Shortell, who has been my conscience for a shocking number of years, as well as the world's best drinking buddy, Josh Eastin. In addition, the women faculty members of the criminology and criminal justice department have all been such important sources of advice and support over the years, and I am especially thankful to Mauri, Katie, and Kelsey (a.k.a. the other founding members of the Fire Club). Y'all are my *women in proximity* (read the book) who have propelled me forward while also reminding me to not take anything too seriously—thank you.

I am very appreciative of the efforts of my three graduate research assistants during my years at PSU. Each of these students contributed to the success of this book in their own way, and it would be a lesser project without their help. Heidi Busche, Stephanie Hawke, and Mike FitzGerald (a.k.a. the Beaker to my Dr. Bunsen Honeydew)—thank you all so much. It was a pleasure working with all of you, and I am so hopeful for your bright futures.

I also want to recognize the many outstanding graduate and undergraduate students at PSU whose curiosity, eagerness to learn, and willingness to question inspires me every day; I feel so lucky to have known you. I'm not going to name anyone in particular because there've been a lot of you and I don't want to risk forgetting someone, so just know this: if you were a student of mine—particularly in my comparative gender and politics class—your efforts, questions, and curiosity inspired this book.

While this book was rolling around in my head, my university allowed me to spend a quarter teaching abroad in Rosario, Argentina. Thank you to Beba Nelida de Juano—the outstanding site director—for welcoming me and making my job fun and painless. I also want to thank the intrepid bunch of Oregon students who joined me in Argentina: Adriane

Ackerman, Robbie Edwards-Farewell, Robert Grosvenor, Paul Jackson, and Marcy Silverman. That trip would not have been possible without you, and my memories of y'all sweetly wandering around Rosario while drinking mate and administering surveys will always brighten my heart.

In addition, I feel very lucky to be a part of the amazing women and politics scholarly community. Thank you all for creating research that is so good, so thoughtful, and so rigorous while simultaneously being a really sweet group of people—you inspire me and I am proud to call you my colleagues and friends. Many of you saw parts of this book as discussants and panel participants over the years—thank you for your incredibly helpful comments and encouragement.

Many years ago, I won the Carrie Chapman Catt Prize for the initial instincts of this project, and I am forever thankful to Iowa State University and the Carrie Chapman Catt Center for that amazing honor. It meant so much to me—thank you. In addition, my own Mark O. Hatfield School of Government at PSU awarded me several Hatfield Public Service Grants to fund experiments, surveys, and various creative endeavors related to this book; their support was instrumental to this project coming to fruition.

The quality and rigor of this project was dramatically increased thanks to the comments I received after presenting it to outstanding faculty at other institutions. In particular, I want to thank the organizers and participants of the Gender and Corruption Workshop at the University of Gothenburg, the political science department at Oregon State University (especially Rorie Solberg), and the political science department at the University of California, Merced (especially my brilliant and wonderful bestie, Jessica Trounstine).

Speaking of dramatically increasing quality, I am filled with gratitude for the efforts of the three outstanding scholars who participated in my small but mighty book conference: Kris Kanthak, Diana O'Brien, and Leslie Schwindt-Bayer. At the start of the book conference, my book draft was a brief and rambling manifesto, and I was filled with anxiety about its future. After 48 hours with these scholars (and a fair amount of wine), I had an amazing, methodical plan for revisions as well as a new confidence that this project could be a true contribution. Thank you all so much. And an additional hug of gratitude to Leslie, who has given me so much encouragement and several hilariously good times at various conferences around the world.

The team at Oxford University Press is outstanding, and I am so grateful for their help and guidance with making this project all that it could be. I especially want to recognize my editor, Angela Chnapko, who gives the perfect balance of sweet encouragement and practical advice, as well as her assistant, Alexcee Bechthold, and my outstanding copy-editor, Brid Nowlan. I also want to extend my sincere gratitude to the anonymous reviewers who commented on the manuscript draft—your advice was spot on, and you made this book better. Thank you.

In addition, I want to recognize a group of people who were there for me at random yet pivotal moments in the creation of this book—you each caught me in a moment of doubt and inspired me to keep writing. This book would not exist without your support. Many thanks to Mike Lewis-Beck, Kathleen Gallagher Cunningham, Keely Grand, and my sister from another mister, Melanie Green.

I want to also acknowledge my parents. My parents were interesting people who did their best and were each instrumental in my survival. My mother gave me a place to live and money for food and books, and also taught me the value of a strong will. My father taught me the importance of a quick wit and a stiff drink, both of which I continue to appreciate. And both of them taught me to have a healthy skepticism of authority and distaste for social norms which, while not always beneficial for my career, turned out to be beneficial for my confidence and creativity. Wherever they are now, I hope that they know I'm grateful.

There are no words that can express how thankful I am to my little family for their support in writing this book. First, thank you to my mother-in-law Maureen for being such a sweet grandmother to our children and for giving us thousands of hours of loving childcare. Next, thank you to my sister, who is hilarious, kind, and brilliant—I wouldn't have survived the loss of our dad without you, and I love you even when you don't vote. Which will never happen again, but still. And thank you to my husband, Andy. The phrase "thank you" seems so totally inadequate to express my gratitude to you—you are the greatest, and I can't believe how lucky I am to have found you. This book and really my whole career as a scholar would not exist without your many years of selfless support and love. And now, to my daughters: you make me so proud and full of joy that it overwhelms me. You are both completely amazing creatures—don't ever forget that. And other things to never forget: Be kind, ask questions, ride your bike, learn all that you can, disagree, read everything, get enough sleep, remember that goofiness and laughter are critically important, and, most important: Burn. It. Down.

1

Introduction

There are angels among us. These angels are the men who selflessly and whole-heartedly advocate for gender equality. And the particularly angelic ones are those who are legislators, corporate executives, and other leaders who have substantial power and realize that women should have it too. Canadian Prime Minister Justin Trudeau, for example, initially appeared to be an angel when he voluntarily created gender parity in his cabinet and explained his reasoning with a simple "because it's 2015."[1] These angels facilitate women's presence in politics out of a concern for fairness and equality or, in short, because it's the right thing to do.

Because good and evil cannot exist without one another, there are devils too. These devils are the men who actively fight against women's inclusion due to their own misogyny, or "backlash" against women in power due to discomfort with their presence. French legislator Patrick Balkany demonstrated his demonic tendencies in 2012 when, during a presentation by Minister of Housing Cecile Duflot, he wolf-whistled to the point of disrupting her speech. Balkany claimed that his behavior was driven by Duflot's choice of outfit, saying that she wore that particular dress "so that we wouldn't listen to what she was saying."[2] British legislator Austin Mitchell offers another example of blatantly rejecting women's presence in the public sphere. In his Op Ed article for the *Daily Mail* in 2014, he ranted against the use of gender quotas for his Labour party, saying that with more women "the party will be more manageable and reasonable, for apart from obsessive feminism, women MPs are more amenable and

Figure 1.1 A Rational Opportunist in Angel's Clothing
(Prime Minister Justin Trudeau at the Canada Summer Games in 2017).
SOURCE: 2017 Canada Summer Games, CC BY 2.0 (https://creativecommons.org/
licenses/by/2.0), via Wikimedia Commons.

leadable and less objectionable. But it might not make us tougher." He
then went on to express his concerns about how a "family-friendly, gentler
party" would face up to the "Tory hooligans."[3] In short, the devils block
women's access to power and, should a woman fight her way in, the devils
strive to disempower her.

However, while the angels and devils are dramatic and fascinating, neither category accurately represents the majority of men in politics. The
majority of men (and women) in politics are simply rational opportunists;
they are not inherently good or evil. The opportunists have no explicit
objections to women in power, but also do not feel an intrinsic need to
support their equality. Instead, they are focused entirely on maintaining
their own power. There should be no normative shade on their desire to
maintain power—it is simply the rational thing to do. These men—the
rational opportunists—are quite powerful and yet surprisingly under-
studied in the field of women's representation. Existing literature focuses

primarily on the institutional, structural, and cultural factors that impact the descriptive representation of women—that is, the number of women in power. These are all critically important determinants, but they are not the whole story. What we don't know yet is why the group already in power—men—would allow women into the political sphere. That is, given that all governments today are patriarchies and that all political parties have men in a majority of their leadership positions, women's representation should not be thought of as a story driven entirely by overarching contextual factors and women's ambition but also as one driven by the individual choices of male gate-keepers who control the political parties and governments.

This book addresses this gap in the literature through an analysis of men's motivations in facilitating women's presence in politics. In short, I consider the blunt questions of when and why men let the women in. Or, in broader form: Why and under what circumstances do members of the "in" group allow and even encourage members of the "out" group to be in government? I argue that, under certain circumstances, men in power benefit from sharing some of their power with women. Specifically, I suggest that women's presence in government in modern times is dependent upon a calculation of inclusion that weighs the costs and benefits of increasing the presence of women in politics. This calculation becomes particularly apparent when the status quo breaks in such a way that the stereotypes associated with women increase in value; in this scenario, women's presence can be strategically used as a signal of certain positive qualities and characteristics of the party or government. This interpretation of women's presence in power, according to my argument, places a political value on women which generates an incentive for male elites in states and political parties to both recruit them and (at times) embrace their inclusion. Women's descriptive representation, in short, is often driven by the strategic value of having women in power, not the embrace of women's power.

In the remainder of this chapter, I offer a brief overview of the central theory of this book, which I then expand on in chapters 2 and 3. I begin with a brief discussion of the existing literature on women's representation to establish the foundations of what we already know about women's path to political office. Then, I engage the literature on rational incentives that drive political behavior and suggest that the self-interested motivations of gate-keepers should be considered in any analysis of women's descriptive representation. Finally, I present a synopsis of the following chapters of this book and briefly describe the theoretical contributions and empirical examinations presented in an effort which culminates in, hopefully, a new perspective on women's descriptive representation.

EXISTING SCHOLARSHIP: WHAT DRIVES WOMEN'S REPRESENTATION?

In the existing literature on women's descriptive representation, scholars suggest that there are several factors that systematically impact women's electoral success. One of the most examined effects is that of governing institutions and, in particular, the electoral system: there is ample evidence that more women are elected to legislatures under proportional representation (PR) than majoritarian electoral systems (Norris 1985; Rule 1987; Darcy et al. 1994; Matland and Studlar 1996). Other electoral variables, such as party magnitude (Matland 1993) and intraparty competition (Valdini 2012, 2013), are also shown to have a systematic effect on women's success. In addition, there is substantial existing research on the effect of gender quotas on women's representation. Gender quotas, as many scholars demonstrate, have the potential to positively impact women's political presence, but simple existence does not denote effectiveness; the specific design of the quota determines its effectiveness. For example, the inclusion of placement mandates and penalties for noncompliance are two critically important design elements that can dramatically impact whether a quota is either a game-changer or a waste of time (Murray 2004; Schwindt-Bayer 2009). Socioeconomic variables, such as women's average income and participation in the labor force, as well as literacy rates and education levels are also shown to impact women's presence in public office (Norris 1985, 1997; Norris and Lovenduski 1995; Darcy et al. 1994; Matland 1998, 2005; Rosenbluth et al. 2006). Further, there is also evidence that as society modernizes—that is, as the role of religion decreases and the level of economic development increases—traditional gender roles weaken and women are able to join the political sphere is greater numbers (Norris 1985; Rule 1987; Burrell 1994; Norris and Inglehart 2001; Inglehart and Norris 2003; Paxton and Kunovich 2003). And finally, recent research examines the effect of women's political aspirations on their representation and suggests that women's lack of parity in politics is due in part to their low self-confidence. That is, women view themselves as less qualified than men to be politicians and thus have less ambition for public office, thereby removing themselves from consideration even before stepping into the electoral arena (Lawless and Fox 2005, 2010).

However, while the existing literature explains much of the variation in women's descriptive representation, there is a conspicuous absence in existing analyses: where are the men in this story? In the field of women and politics, the motivations and behaviors of men are usually ignored (though the works of Murray, Krook, and Opello (2012), Bjarnegård (2013), and Weeks (2018) are important exceptions) and, while this makes sense—we focus on men in almost every field of political science, so let's at least focus on women in this small area—this field norm has prevented us from seeing an important piece of the puzzle of women's descriptive representation. We live in patriarchies, and thus the power-holders and gatekeepers are primarily men, so how are they responding to the increasing numbers of women who are seeking a role in the political realm? Are they angels who embrace equality and fling open the doors to power? Are they devils who block women's path to power at every turn? Are they powerless against the increasing tide of feminism and thus inadvertently succumbing to the push for power from women? None of these scenarios seem likely; instead, it seems most likely that the power-holders and gatekeepers—the male elites—are primarily concerned with maintaining their own power, and this concern drives their reaction to women's political inclusion. This does not necessarily mean that they actively exclude women but rather that they maintain an awareness that positions of power are finite and temporary, and thus they have no incentive to invite increased competition with an angelic act of inclusion. For most men in power, this is not personal—their behavior is not driven by blatant misogyny—it is instead a rational act of prioritizing their own political well-being above all else and, most of the time, this means that there is no reason to actively recruit or welcome women in power.

THE RATIONAL OPPORTUNIST AND WOMEN'S INCLUSION

When one adjusts the lens of women's representation to include men, the potential use of rational choice theory in understanding men's behavior becomes clear. Under this theoretical perspective, outcomes are driven by individuals maximizing their own utilities, with scarcity and the intervention of institutions, for example, constraining their behaviors. As Levi (1997) points out, the central complication in using this theoretical lens to describe the world is that sometimes it can be difficult to determine what exactly would maximize an individual's utility (p. 24). In other words, if one assumes that actors will behave in a way that is consistently driven by their preferences, then the trick is to determine what those preferences are and how they are ordered. When one is considering elections, however, this complication is minimized; in the electoral context, one can safely assume that, almost always, the top preference is to win the election (Downs 1957; Strøm 1990; Müller and Strøm 1999). Thus, if we apply the principles of rational choice theory to male behavior regarding women's representation, male elites should only have an interest in including more women in the political sphere if it somehow contributes to helping the male elites either maintain or increase their own power. In other words, expecting a male elite to be an angel who saintly sacrifices his own power for a woman's gain or a devil who restricts the power of women just out of spite and malice will usually be incorrect; under most circumstances, rational opportunists care much more about winning than women's inclusion (or anything else), and thus their actions on this front should reflect their desire to win above all else.

Rational choice theory plays a prominent role in several important studies of elite and party behavior. Weingast (1997) offers an example of this line of thought in his analysis of the behavior of political officials. He argues that politicians choose to respect citizens' rights depending on whether it is in their interest to abide by them; in other words, elected officials respect the limits of the constitution on their behavior if they fear losing their jobs. Thus, it is not a beautiful commitment to democracy that causes politicians to behave in accordance with the constitution— after all, they are not angels. Whether or not they do so depends on whether it is in their own interest. Fenno (1978) offers a similar theoretical perspective in his ground-breaking work on the behavior of US legislators. He finds that, above all, legislators want to be re-elected, and this drives them to allocate their resources in whatever way will make that possible. Thus, rather than stay in Washington, DC, and focus on national policy matters, US legislators spend a significant amount of their time, money, and attention on their constituency and "home style" because it is in their self-interest to do so. Murray (2010) also engages rational choice theory in her analysis of the ways in which French political parties responded to the compulsory gender quota law adopted in 2000. She explains that because the gender quota necessitated that some political parties unseat incumbents in order to follow the law, certain parties realized that it was not in their best interest to abide by it. Thus, they violated the quota law because they felt that losing male incumbents would be more costly to their electoral future than running fewer women candidates, thereby prioritizing the party's electoral success above all else. While all of these analyses are different, they all share a similar finding: elected officials want to win more elections, and their desire to win future elections drives their behavior.

The desire to win is a crucial element in our understanding of the political behavior of elected officials and should thus be considered in analyses of the descriptive representation of women as well. And when one does engage this theoretical perspective, its value is immediately clear: if we assume that men are maximizing their individual likelihoods of winning, there is little reason to expect that people in power (men) would welcome competitors (women) to the political playing field, because it would be counter to their self-interest. And yet, there are many examples of male elites recruiting women into government by adopting gender quotas or even mentoring women candidates. Are those men acting irrationally? On the contrary, their behavior suggests that they are somehow benefiting from the inclusion of women. I argue that this factor—the benefit men can receive from women's inclusion—is a primary driver of women's descriptive representation. Specifically, I suggest that male elites employ an "inclusion calculation" of sorts to estimate the potential benefit of adding more women to their political party or government, as well as the potential costs to both their own access to power and their party's electoral future. This calculation, I argue, is not necessarily conscious or deliberate but is happening nonetheless; it is the rational response of men in power to the presence of new competitors. Thus, even when there is a strategic benefit to including more women, this theory implies that male elites will only grant women minimal levels of power and access. Again, not because they are devils, but because power is a zero-sum game, and thus it is rational for the current elites to protect their own power rather than share it. In other words, the unprecedented increases in women's descriptive representation during the past few decades may be due, in part, to the benefit women's representation brings to men in power. And because of that, one should not expect the increased presence of women to also trigger increased power for women.

Throughout this book, I frame the presence of women as candidates and legislators as being the result of a strategic calculation of elites. I present several variables that, I argue, make up the equation that determines whether or not elites will facilitate women's increased inclusion and refer to each variable as a potential "cost" or "benefit" of women's inclusion. I determine the general values of the variables by analyzing the institutional and social context of the legislative election and note that, under most circumstances, the values of these variables either stay constant across multiple elections or change slowly over time. This is, quite obviously, all conjecture; there is no direct test of this theory of the inclusion calculation, and there is also no way to determine actual numeric values of these variables. Further, under normal conditions, it is difficult to see even any indirect evidence that elites are using any sort of strategic calculation. However, when the status quo breaks and the party or government begins to lose substantial legitimacy, I argue that the elite strategy surrounding women's inclusion becomes most visible. In this moment of the broken status quo, the values of the variables in the inclusion calculation change rapidly, which in turn triggers elites to rapidly change course on women's inclusion. This moment, therefore, reveals the relationship between elite strategy and women's presence in the political realm; when elites believe that women's inclusion can benefit their electoral futures, women's inclusion quickly increases.

While there are many conceivable events that break the status quo and drive down legitimacy, I focus on two in this book: first, after the disclosure of a massive corruption scandal in government in which multiple high-ranking state or party officials are accused of using public office for private gain; second, in a hybrid regime, and particularly one that is degrading the remaining elements of democracy, such as reducing civil rights or blatantly biasing electoral outcomes. In these contexts, the government and/or political party is losing legitimacy due to a public perception that they are corrupt, greedy, power-hungry, and/or subverting the rules. In turn, the benefits and costs of women's inclusion change, and change quickly and dramatically. Instead of seeing women as simply potential competitors vying for power, I argue that elites in these environments see women's inclusion as a relatively low-cost way to increase their legitimacy and maintain their hold on power.

In the context of rapidly declining legitimacy, the stereotypical personality traits associated with women potentially become an asset; this is the moment when citizens are looking for evidence that the greed and malfeasance will soon end and be replaced with stability and honesty, and thus women's assumed traits increase in value. While the symbolic meaning of women varies across citizens, countries, and cultural spheres of influence, some of the most common traits associated with women are honesty, inclusiveness, and a natural affinity for democracy (Alexander and Andersen 1993; Kahn 1994; Huddy and Capelos 2002; Lawless 2004; Goetz 2007; Dolan 2010). These common stereotypes, I argue, not only affect the electoral fortunes of the women associated with them but are also powerful enough to cause citizens to view women's presence as a signal about the institutions in which they participate. Rather than guilt by association, this is feminization by association. In other words, a benefit that women's descriptive representation potentially brings to men in power is the association with feminine stereotypical traits and behaviors; by including women in their governments or political parties, citizens assume that the associated institution will be more honest, inclusive, and democratic. Thus, for male elites to maintain power in this context, associating their party or government with women becomes a rational strategy; because women are strongly associated with the stereotypes that will signal voters of change, democracy, and honesty, the electoral benefit of their inclusion potentially outweighs the cost to elites' zero-sum conception of power.

While I argue that the symbolism of women's presence *can* be valuable to the state and political elites, it is critical to emphasize that its value is temporary, context-dependent, and possibly not enough to outweigh the costs of inclusion. Existing scholarship demonstrates that feminine traits are not typically viewed as being essential to leadership. In fact, just the opposite is true—there is substantial evidence that many feminine personality traits are "incongruent" with the usual citizen conceptualization of the ideal leader. Voters typically prefer their leaders to exhibit stereotypically masculine traits such as being assertive, competitive, forceful, and dominant (Eagly and Karau 2002; Eagly and Carli 2007; Koenig et al. 2011). Thus, under many circumstances, associating the party with women will not necessarily be a winning strategy. Further, even when feminine traits increase in value, the institutional and social environment may make women's inclusion too costly for the party to see any real electoral benefit. For example, if the electoral system generates a high incentive to cultivate a personal vote, then incumbency becomes especially valuable to the party. In this particular institutional environment, displacing male incumbents in order to run more women candidates will be quite costly to the party, thereby making women's increased inclusion a poor strategy for a rational opportunist. This is why it is important to understand the benefit (or cost) of associating with women's stereotyped traits as a single variable in an inclusion calculation with several other variables; no single factor should drive a party gate-keeper to include more women, but rather a weighing of the many costs and benefits for the party as well as the individual. In short, no matter the circumstances, one should not expect the benefit of women's inclusion to *automatically* outweigh the costs.

In addition to the value of women legislators as symbols of honesty and democracy, it seems that the strategic use of women's inclusion is a rational strategy for two other reasons: first, the inclusion of more women candidates or the adoption of a gender quota—that is, a commitment to increasing the presence of women in politics—serves as a quick and simple substitute for addressing the systemic failure(s) that caused either the massive corruption scandal or the slow death of democracy in a hybrid regime. Elites would prefer *not* to undertake profound reform because the changes will likely undermine their own power, and thus the appearance of action through either a legislated quota or a dramatic increase in women candidates is a better choice. Second, the strategic use of women's representation is also a wise strategy because, even when women are included in the political sphere at record numbers and with record levels of power, all countries continue to be patriarchies. Therefore, the inclusion of women carries less of a potential threat than the inclusion of men from traditionally excluded groups; in other words, women are the safest "other" to include. Unlike an under-represented ethnic group, for example, women's inclusion carries no threat that they will take over the regime or even a region of the country and declare independence. Instead, the guaranteed outcome is that women will participate in and maintain the regime and will not use their minimal levels of power as a foothold to overthrow and transition to a matriarchy.[4]

At this point, it is important to emphasize a critical element of my argument: just because women are used strategically, this does not mean that they are unqualified. It is absolutely not the case that, when a political elite decides his party could benefit from being associated with women, he just pops outside and invites the first woman he sees to run for office. The idea that there was a lack of qualified women available was a popular explanation for women's under-representation in the twentieth century and for much of that century it was indeed true. But it is no longer true today, no matter the country. Even in those developing states where women's literacy lags behind that of men, there are still substantial numbers of (wealthy) women completing higher education, obtaining degrees, and getting involved in politics at the local level. There is no shortage of qualified women and thus, even when political elites decide to strategically increase their presence, one should not assume that women are less fit to serve than men. That being said, one should anticipate that rational opportunists will be strategic about exactly which women they choose. There is an obvious incentive here to, when possible, select women who are inexperienced because they will be easier to control. For example, it may appear to be a publicity stunt when a party selects a porn star for their candidate lists—such as Ilona Staller in Italy—or a respectful gesture to the family to select the wife, sister, or daughter of a former elected representative who passes away in office, but these are also savvy political moves that lower the cost of women's inclusion in the eyes of elites. By choosing a woman who has little political experience, elites increase the likelihood that she will be dependent upon them for guidance, and thus she is less of a threat to the existing power structure. In addition, there is also a clear incentive to select women who are outwardly supportive of the patriarchy. As Derks et al. (2016) explain in their analysis of the conditions under which men select women for leadership positions:

> Selecting a woman who explicitly legitimizes the current gender hierarchy (e.g., by denying that gender discrimination exists) over a woman who seeks to improve opportunities for other women further serves to protect the status quo in which most positions of power are held by men. (page 463)

Thus, while it would be incorrect to assume that male elites are forced to select unqualified women due to the lack of qualified women available, it is not incorrect to suspect that elites may seek out women who are inexperienced or have traditional ideas about gender roles.

This is also a good moment to explain my terminology. Throughout this book, I use the phrase "elites" or "male elites" to refer to men in positions of decision-making power, and I imply that these men have the unilateral capacity to authorize women's entrance into the political sphere. This is problematic for two central reasons. First, it minimizes women's agency. That is, rather than suggesting that the story of women's representation is due to either neutral institutions, societal factors, or women themselves, I over-emphasize the power of men in women's representation. This is a conscious decision and is driven by the goal of drawing attention to what I believe is the often overlooked role of patriarchy in mainstream gender and politics literature. It is an exaggeration to imply that all of women's political activity has been authorized by men; women's activists, women candidates, and women elites have fought and won, and I do not mean to minimize their accomplishments. But I also want to reflect on the many activists, candidates, and elites who have fought and lost—and I would assert that this group of women is much larger than the group of winners. By pretending that those women have just as much agency as men, we imply that their loss was all their fault, when indeed, because we live in a patriarchal system that values the contributions, decisions, and ideas of men more than women, it continues to be challenging for women to achieve positions of power. Thus, while my focus on the strategies of male elites purposefully undervalues the role of women's agency, I would argue that women's agency has been erroneously over-stated in the existing literature on representation.

The other problem with my conception of male elites as the unilateral gate-keepers of entry to the political sphere is that it ignores the fact that there are women elites as well. This is again a purposeful exaggeration, designed to call attention to what I believe is a mistaken assumption in existing literature. Too often, women serving in political office are assumed to be just as powerful as their male colleagues, but this ignores the reality of a patriarchy; we cannot assume that women have equal access to power in a system designed to privilege and maintain men's power. While there are some women who have become, for example, leaders of major political parties, the number is so small that their access to power is limited. In her analysis of party leadership in parliamentary democracies, O'Brien (2015) notes that of the 441 party leaders in her primarily western European data set, only 14% are women. Further, her results suggest that women are more likely to become leaders of parties if the party is minor, in opposition, and losing seat share; in other words, when power is limited, women are most likely to gain access to leadership positions. In addition, Krook (2009) acknowledges the continuing dominance of men in the political sphere in her research on gender quota adoption. Building on the work of Schmidt (2003), she explains that:

> even in cases where a large number of women do support quotas, their proposals rarely gain consideration until at least one well-placed elite man embraces them and pressures his own party, or his own colleagues in parliament, to approve quotas for women. (page 22)

Thus, because there are still so few women in positions with real power, and none with unilateral power, as well as to draw attention to the continuing power of the patriarchy in women's political fates, I build this book on the foundational assumption that the gate-keepers are male.

SYNOPSIS OF THE BOOK

I begin this book with two chapters devoted to establishing the theoretical foundations of my argument. In chapter 2, I consider the existing literature on elite strategy and women's representation and build a conceptual framework of the competing individual and partisan motivations that rational opportunists face when contemplating the addition of women to the political sphere under status quo conditions. I build, in short, the inclusion calculation. I argue that women's inclusion rests on a calculation of costs and benefits of their presence and further, that this calculation changes dramatically when there is a break in the status quo that triggers a substantial loss of legitimacy. In the context of declining legitimacy, women's "role incongruity" potentially becomes a benefit and, depending on the other variables in the equation, this is often enough to trigger rational opportunists to strategically increase women's inclusion.

In chapter 3, I continue to develop my central theory on the strategic use of women in politics by focusing on the *incongruity benefit* and its mechanism of feminization by association. I highlight the powerful and enduring role of gender stereotypes in societies across the world and, to that end, I offer an original survey that examines the traits that are typically associated with male versus female legislators. I find evidence that the incongruency between leadership norms and traditional feminine stereotypes continues—people do not seem to believe that women have the necessary traits to rule alone—but also that there seems to be a strong sentiment that women bring a voice of honesty and fairness to governance. Building from this premise, I then argue that rational opportunists strategically increase women's presence in a party or government when they see a benefit to associating with symbols of increased honesty or democracy. In short, when an institution is seen as untrustworthy, elites are more likely to increase women's inclusion in an effort to change the perception of it, thereby generating legitimacy for the political party or regime.

The empirical chapters of this book each examine a political context that should, according to my theory, increase the value of women's presence. There is no survey or other direct test that can by itself establish the validity of my central claim, and thus my strategy is to offer several different types of indirect tests that, particularly when viewed together, suggest a clear trend. In chapter 4, I examine the first of the two contexts where the inclusion calculation should be visible: the aftermath of a massive corruption scandal. I argue that elites have an incentive to strategically increase the presence of women candidates in this environment in order to associate themselves and their party with stereotypical feminine traits but that this incentive is not always enough to trigger inclusion. I then offer three analyses to examine the conditions under which elites increase the presence of women candidates on party lists. First, I begin with an original analysis of candidate selection in Spain and Portugal and offer evidence that political parties recruit and run more women candidates in high-profile positions after a massive scandal breaks. Next, I consider candidate selection in Ireland, which also endured a series of massive political scandals shortly before an election but, unlike Spain and Portugal, elites did not respond by increasing the presence of women. Finally, I examine the electoral success of women's candidates in post-scandal environments and offer a large-N regression analysis of legislative electoral results over a period of 20 years.

In chapter 5, I continue my analysis of the effect of corruption scandals on elite behavior, but I consider the circumstances under which the adoption of a gender quota—rather than simply increasing the number of women candidates on party lists—becomes the optimal method of inclusion for elites. I argue that the prevalence of gender quotas today demonstrates that elites see an advantage to this particular method of inclusion and suggest several reasons why a quota offers the benefits of feminization while simultaneously limiting some of the costs of women's inclusion. I assert that the gender quota potentially allows elites more control over women's presence and power than any other method of inclusion and thus, under some circumstances, elites can engage this method without suffering any loss to their own power. In addition, I present case study analyses of the adoption of legislated gender quotas in two countries—Italy and Argentina—and argue that quota adoption was driven by both the benefit of strategically associating with women in the post-scandal environment as well as the particular advantages of this method of inclusion in these contexts.

In chapter 6, I examine the context of hybrid regimes—also known as pseudodemocracies—and argue that the incentive to mimic democracies in this regime type triggers governments to increase the legislative representation of women, particularly when the state is removing civil rights. That is, because women are stereotyped as being naturally more honest, cooperative, and democratic, women's descriptive representation is strategically manipulated to signal a commitment to these ideals. I test this theory through a cross-sectional, time-series model that utilizes the election results of 27 countries over 16 years and find evidence that women's legislative presence in hybrid regimes correlates with a loss of civil rights. Finally, I offer case studies of Ethiopia and Bangladesh, two hybrid regimes that experienced a dramatic reduction in civil rights while simultaneously adopting gender quotas and increasing the presence of women in politics. The analysis suggests that governments proactively add women to their legislatures both shortly before and during periods of civil rights removal.

In chapter 7, I offer the implications of my findings as well as suggestions for future research. Because the findings of this book suggest that women's political presence can be a strategic tool used by male gate-keepers to maintain power, one of the key implications of this project is that scholars who analyze women's descriptive representation should engage more with the strategies of male elites in their analyses. That is, our understanding of the drivers of women's representation should continue to include institutions, structural status, cultural norms, and women's ambition, but the costs and benefits of women's inclusion to the men in power should also be included in our analyses. In addition, my findings also suggest that the often-assumed relationship between women's presence and democracy is not causal and thus that scholars in any field should not employ women's political presence as a signal of good governance or democracy. Finally, I suggest that scholars use more caution when their findings demonstrate a correlation between women's low confidence and our descriptive representation. We can encourage women to be more ambitious—to lean in!—but also temper our expectations with the fact that we live in patriarchies. The troubling reality is that the gate-keepers are male and we are all playing under rules that privilege men, and thus we cannot simply "try harder" in order to gain access. Instead, by increasing our awareness of the patriarchal political arena, we can build strategies for inclusion that consciously navigate—and slowly undermine—the current reality of women's oppression.

The Calculation
of Women's Inclusion

From the perspective of rational choice theory, there is a clear disincentive to being inclusive. If one welcomes nontraditional candidates to the political arena, then the pool of future competitors is increased; in other words, if one is basing the choice of inclusion on simply the cost of competing with more political actors for resources and power, then it is rational for elites to prevent members of marginalized groups from entering the political sphere. And yet, while this disincentive to inclusion hovers in their calculations, there are many other factors that rational party elites weigh when determining whether or not to include women on their party lists. After all, whether they have the ultimate goal of increasing the power of their elites and/or of implementing favorable policy, the fundamental goal of the political party is to win elections (Downs 1957; Strøm 1990; Müller and Strøm 1999). The party elites, therefore, have an incentive to develop a dynamic and responsive approach to candidate selection in which they are calculating the multiple costs and benefits of inclusion, all in an effort to select candidates with the maximum potential to win and increase the electability of the party as a whole. Existing literature has yet to map the specific costs and benefits of women's inclusion from the perspective of the party elites, and thus this chapter offers a new approach to understanding candidate selection decisions. In it, I present a conceptual framework of the competing individual and partisan motivations that male rational opportunists face when building the party lists of candidates and offer a method of tracking the likely costs and benefits of women's inclusion under various institutional, political, and social conditions.

Building from the foundational work of Müller and Strøm (1999) on the general decision-making process of party leaders as well as the work of Murray et al. (2012) on party pragmatism and women's inclusion, I conceptualize the rational opportunist party elite as being driven primarily by a desire to maximize both individual and partisan future success. Because these leaders are neither angels nor devils, their preferences on women's inclusion are neither simple nor clear-cut. Their decision to include women rests instead, I argue, on a calculation of costs and benefits, and these costs and benefits change depending on the institutional and political environment; this is, in short, the "inclusion calculation," and I view it as crucial for understanding women's descriptive representation. Specifically, I present five factors that are recognized in the literature as affecting the likelihood that women candidates are included on party lists. While these factors are not explicitly discussed in existing literature as "costs and benefits" in the mind of the rational opportunist selector, they fit naturally into a framework of calculation. The first factor is the *displacement cost*, which concerns the potential negative impact of replacing incumbents with women candidates. The second factor is the *threat cost*, which refers to the personal fear of the party elites that the newly included women candidates will someday undermine the power or resources of the current, male elite. The third factor is the *incongruity cost*, which concerns the potentially negative electoral impact of having women on the party list due to their association with stereotypically feminine personality traits. The fourth factor is the *domestic responsiveness cost or benefit*, which refers to the potential electoral reward or punishment for responding to a social movement or other societal group that is calling for the increased inclusion of women. Finally, I discuss the *international responsiveness cost or benefit*, which concerns the tangible benefits offered by international organizations (IOs) in response to the increased presence of women in politics, as well as the potential societal backlash to responding to international pressure. In addition, while not a part of the inclusion calculation,

I consider the effect of *women in proximity* to the rational opportunist. I argue that sometimes, though not always, women in proximity can tip the balance in favor of inclusion, particularly when the inclusion calculation offers a result of nearly equal costs and benefits.

After outlining the implicit costs and benefits of women's inclusion under normal conditions, I consider the effect of changing political conditions on the results of the inclusion calculation. I suggest that a break in the status quo offers a rare glimpse of the calculation of women's inclusion: rather than the relatively static calculation found under normal conditions, the status quo break changes the values of multiple variables, which in turn triggers a more dramatic change in women's inclusion. Specifically, I argue that when a change in the status quo entails a loss of legitimacy for the government or political party, then the incongruity cost has the potential to partially transition to an *incongruity benefit* which, in turn, increases the likelihood of women's political inclusion.

While it should be possible to apply this general conceptual framework to any leader, I focus my analysis on the expected motivations and behaviors of a political party leader. This particular actor is one of the most empowered in the political process. As Strøm and Müller (1999) explain in their analysis of party elite decision-making, "Leadership frequently means making hard choices. In modern democracies, the leaders who make these choices are highly likely to be party politicians or indeed party leaders" (p. 1). Further, party leaders—at both the national and local level—tend to have the most control over the inclusion of women in the political sphere because of their role as the "selectorate"—the group of elites who decide which aspirants will actually become candidates on the party roster, and whose importance is hard to overstate. As Hazan and Rahat (2010) explain, "in the majority of democratic nations, in a majority of the parties, selection is equal to election" (p. 11). Women's election to office, therefore, is strongly dependent upon whether women are selected to run as candidates by the elites. In the explanation of the inclusion calculation variables in the following section, I focus on this single method of inclusion—the addition of women candidates to the party lists by the selectorate—so as to make the initial conceptualization of the inclusion calculation as straightforward as possible.[1]

THE DISPLACEMENT COST

The bounded nature of power makes the inclusion of a new group a challenge for any elite; after all, whenever someone moves up in the ranks, someone else must move down. In particular, when an elite is faced with the prospect of removing a proven winner—an incumbent—and replacing him with a new candidate, there is a clear cost, no matter the gender of the new candidate. There is consistent evidence that incumbency has a powerful effect on the likelihood of a candidate's electoral success (Gelman and King 1990; Ansolabehere et al. 2000; Ashworth and Bueno de Mesquita 2008), and thus this is frequently cited as a reason why women (who are often non-incumbents) are not winning legislative seats at the same rate as men (Schwindt-Bayer 2005). Further, while incumbency is arguably the most valuable candidate trait, there are other candidate traits that an elite may be hesitant to remove, such as a candidate with local roots or a surname with a positive political history. Thus, it is clear that displacing an incumbent or a candidate with potentially valuable traits is a potential expense, and one that weighs heavily enough on party elites to sometimes prevent the inclusion of women.

However, while this expense has the potential to be powerful, the displacement cost varies by institutional design; it is not, in other words, equally costly to remove an incumbent legislator in the closed-list PR system of Spain, for example, as it is in the majoritarian electoral system of the United Kingdom. The relationship between electoral system and the candidate selection of women is nothing new; existing literature consistently demonstrates that if a country uses PR to elect its legislators, then party leaders are more likely to choose women to run as candidates. If, however, a majoritarian system is used, then women are less likely to be chosen as candidates (Gallagher and Marsh 1988; Darcy et al. 1994; Ware 1996; Goetz 2003; Norris 2004). The causal explanation for this relationship is usually that in PR systems, party elites prefer to present a "balanced ticket" that signals inclusion and satisfies factions within the party (Gallagher and Marsh 1988; Norris 2004), while in majoritarian systems, the winner-take-all natures of the system drives elites to instead select candidates with a mainstream and traditional appeal and thus avoid any candidates that they perceive as more electorally "risky" (Matland 1993).

It seems, however, that in addition to the incentive to present a "balanced ticket" in PR, it is simply easier to find room on the party lists for newcomers in this electoral system. That is, the party magnitude—or the anticipated number of seats that the party will win in each district—changes the cost of adding more women to the candidate lists. As Matland (1993) explains, if the party magnitude equals one, then there is the potential for a zero-sum game: in this scenario, the party only has one likely winner, and thus elites have a strong incentive to both maximize appeal (by running a candidate with local roots, for example) and prevent the displacement of a proven past winner. Therefore, it is not just a desire to balance the lists that drives women's inclusion in PR, but also a lower displacement cost due to the (typically) higher party magnitude.

In addition, the incentive to cultivate a "personal vote" also impacts the displacement cost. A personal vote is that part of a candidate's vote that is based on his or her individual characteristics or record (Cain et al. 1987), and the incentive to cultivate a personal vote is determined by the electoral system (Carey and Shugart 1995). In a system that generates a high personal vote, the personal traits of the candidates matter to the voters. In other words, this electoral system creates an incentive for voters to seek candidate-specific information, and thus the political parties have an incentive to run candidates with particular attributes that will appeal to voters, such as incumbency or local roots (Shugart et al. 2005). In this electoral context, therefore, displacing a candidate or incumbent with personal vote-earning attributes (PVEA) will be potentially more costly to the political party because they are removing a candidate who has characteristics with proven appeal. In a system with a low level of personal vote, however, the displacement cost is lower. In this context, the voters are not as concerned with the personal traits of candidates, and thus party elites can remove incumbents or a candidate with local roots and replace them with women without being as concerned that they are endangering the electoral success of their party.[2]

The displacement cost also varies based on the political context. After a negative political event—such as a corruption scandal that involves several legislators—it is potentially beneficial to the party for the selectors to displace incumbents. In this scenario, the elite are preemptively "throwing the bastards out" in an effort to convince the voters that they don't have to. Klašnja (2015) examines the potential for voters to respond negatively to the incumbency cue—referred to as the incumbency disadvantage—and finds evidence that if voters perceive high levels of corruption and the potential to increase corruption further as time in office extends, incumbency becomes a curse rather than a blessing. Thus in a political context with significant corruption that is upsetting the voters, the cost of replacing incumbents with women is lower than in a positive context.

In a similar vein, a negative political event may also trigger a "natural" decrease in the displacement cost because incumbents may choose not to run again. That is, if the desirability of the seat decreases, then male incumbents may not want to remain in office, and thus space opens up for women. Existing literature demonstrates a powerful impact of seat desirability on women's successful ascension to leadership positions, offering evidence that negative party performance or crisis increases the likelihood that women will become party leaders (Beckwith 2013; O'Brien 2015). Further, this logic underlies the growing scholarship on the "glass cliff" phenomena, in which women are more likely to be selected for leadership of organizations that are experiencing unprecedented challenges, in part because men do not want these more risky leadership positions (Ryan and Haslam 2005, 2007; Ryan et al. 2016). Similar logic could be applied to legislative seats as well; if a party is in crisis, then male incumbents may jump ship to other parties (depending, of course, on the available options in the party system), which in turn creates open seats for women at no displacement cost.

THE THREAT COST

While the displacement cost is rooted in the potential harm to the success of the party as a whole, the threat cost is personal. It refers to the personal calculation of an elite regarding the likelihood that the inclusion of women will impact his access to power and his career trajectory. Every political actor is a potential threat to an elite, but actors from groups that are typically subjugated are a particularly dangerous threat for two reasons. First they (both women and candidates from other under-represented groups) may appeal to voters and other elites because they are perceived as bringing something new to the table. As I argue throughout this book, usually this "something new" from women is based on communal stereotypes and is not enough to overpower negative assumptions about such candidates but, under certain circumstances, the increase in women's value also increases their threat potential. Second, women's inclusion is a particularly unnerving threat because it has the potential to induce a systemic overhaul of the patriarchy. Let me be clear: I am not arguing that any political party elite is explicitly thinking, "If I increase women candidates, I may induce the loss of the patriarchy." This is an implicit threat, but as such, is no less powerful.

Existing literature offers consistent findings that the engagement of a traditionally excluded group—women—in positions of potential power is a threat to the system of male dominance. In her analysis of harassment, Berdahl (2007) argues that men have a desire to protect or enhance their sex-based social status when they feel threatened. She explains that political institutions such as legislatures emphasize sex differences by "valorizing male dominance and privilege," which in turn exacerbates men's motivation to protect their privileged status (p. 646). In other words, because men are a "high status" group, they are "more biased in favor of their ingroups because they seek to maintain their positive social identity vis-à-vis the low-status group" (Bettencourt and Bartholow 1998, p. 762). In her analysis of gender quota resistance, Krook (2016) also discusses this phenomenon. She explains that " . . . while constrained by the pressures of public opinion, as well as the formal letter of the law, dominant groups benefit from rules, practices, and norms that support and justify their position of privilege" (p. 270). There is an incentive, in other words, for men (as members of the dominant group) to normalize and support women's exclusion from politics, because women's inclusion is an implicit threat to the privileged status of men.

I argue that the most powerful institutional determinant of the threat cost is the distance of women's inclusion point from the elite in power. If elites can increase women's presence in the political sphere by including them at significantly lower levels of power, then that long distance to power induces a low threat cost. In other words, it will take many years and substantial effort for those women to threaten that elite's personal power, and thus it is of little concern. Further, women's presence at lower levels of power is unlikely to undermine the status of men (at least in the near future), and thus there is little concern that they will undermine systemic male dominance. If, on the other hand, elites are increasing women's presence in positions close to real power or even at the elite level itself, this indicates a high threat cost. At this level of inclusion, women are both a patriarchal systemic threat and a personal new competitor to the elite, and thus the cost of their inclusion is at its highest.

In the context of legislative candidate selection by party elites, the distance of women's inclusion point to elite power is profoundly impacted by the level of decentralization in the candidate selection process. When the candidate selection process is centralized—that is, the national-level political party elites determine the candidates, perhaps with some local-level input but the national-level maintains decision-making authority—this maximizes the distance from the inclusion point to the elites. It will take these women substantial time and effort to move up the ranks to those few national-level elite positions, and thus their potential threat will affect a different set of elites than the one engineering their inclusion. However, when candidate selection is decentralized, several groups of local-level elites around the country are the primary decision-makers on who will become a party candidate, and thus the distance from inclusion point to elite is much shorter. The party ranks are potentially easier to rise through when there are multiple local-level leadership points, and thus the new rank-and-file women candidates will be able to enter these local elite positions faster and with more ease, thereby becoming personal threats in the near future.

Existing literature on the impact of the centralization of candidate selection procedures demonstrates a consistent relationship between centralization and women's inclusion. If the selection process is centralized with national-level party elites, then women are more likely to be selected as candidates. If, however, primaries or local-level party elites make the nomination decisions, then there will be fewer women candidates. The explanation for this relationship in existing literature is that the national level is more "concerned" with gender equity than elites at the local level (Leijenaar 1993; Matland and Studlar 1996). However, Hinojosa (2012) argues that centralized candidate selection undermines the importance of local power monopolies. In other words, national level party elites make their decisions based on "electoral concerns and expected outcomes," while local-level elites tend to draw from their traditional networks of power (p. 54). This argument supports the concept of a threat cost: the rational opportunists at the local-level draw from the traditional networks of men not because they are misogynist, but rather because they are in close proximity to new entrants to the political arena. And these new entrants are close enough to be a threat to their personal power and overarching dominance in the short term. The national-level selectorate, on the other hand, has a lower threat cost and thus, can prioritize the reputation and general success of the party.

THE INCONGRUITY COST

There is substantial evidence that feminine personality traits are viewed as "incongruent" with the usual citizen conceptualization of the ideal leader. That is, voters typically prefer their leaders to exhibit stereotypically masculine or "agentic" traits such as being assertive, confident, forceful, and dominant, not the communal traits stereotypically associated with women (Eagly and Karau 2002; Eagly and Carli 2007; Koenig et al. 2011). And, when women do demonstrate these traditionally masculine traits, there is a backlash against them due to their violation of expected gendered behaviors (Rudman 1998; Eagly and Karau 2002; Heilman and Okimoto 2007; Rudman et al. 2012). These cultural expectations are not unique to the United States. Sczesney et al. (2004) offer evidence from Australia, India, and Germany that the "think-manager-think-male" phenomena—which was first noted by Schein (1975)—continues to be a powerful influence in the minds of voters across the world. One of the most profound consequences of this is that women's leadership is delegitimized—that is, the belief that women do not typically have the personality traits that are necessary for good leadership undermines the power and electability of women leaders. In other words, there is an expectation that women leaders will fall short due to their assumed personality traits, and thus citizens are more likely to perceive them as ineffective leaders (Vial et al. 2016). Thus, the view held by some voters that a woman candidate has traits that are incongruous with good leadership is a potential expense included in the elite calculation of women's inclusion.

Similar to the other costs, however, this is not the same across all systems. Instead, the institutional structure, the level of bias against women in society, and the ideological position of the political party or government determine its intensity. Specifically, if the electoral system includes a personal vote, then the expense depends on the level of bias in that particular society. If the culture of the country is highly biased—a substantial number of people admit to preferring male leaders over female ones—then the personal vote will negatively affect the electoral success of women (Valdini 2013). That is, because an electoral system with a personal vote encourages or even requires voters to base their vote on the personal traits of candidates, the electoral rules encourage the biased citizenry to activate their prejudice when casting a ballot. This, in turn, increases the incongruity cost: party elites will be concerned that the negative response to women candidates will affect the success of the party, and thus their presence will be seen as costlier. If, however, there is no personal vote or if the citizens express low levels of bias, then the incongruity cost decreases: the voters in these countries are either less likely to view women as antithetical to leadership *or* the electoral system prevents them from engaging their antiquated views as a basis of their vote. Either way, rational opportunists will be more likely to run women candidates because the cost of their inclusion is lower. Following the same logic, the ideological position of the political party should also affect the incongruity expense due to the association of right-wing parties with the more traditional (and biased) understanding of gender. Right-wing party elites are aware that their voters tend to embrace a more traditional approach to gender roles, and thus the incongruity cost is higher for them than it is for left-wing rational opportunists.

THE DOMESTIC RESPONSIVENESS COST OR BENEFIT

When a social movement or women's group generates a demand for increased women's inclusion in government, a new potential cost or benefit enters the elite calculus on women's inclusion. Existing literature describes women's groups as potentially mobilizing grassroots women's movements and/or coalitions of multiple women's organizations that can pressure elites to increase women's participation by adopting a gender quota (Beckwith 2003; Baldez 2004; Kang and Tripp 2018). Further, existing literature also emphasizes the potential for the "contagion" of gender quotas in a party system. Contagion is a process by which a small, fringe party adopts a gender quota, which in turn spurs the larger parties to also adopt voluntary gender quotas (Matland and Studlar 1996; Caul 2001; Davidson-Schmich 2006). The underlying logic in both of these scenarios is that of pressure: when women's social movements or women's organizations call for quota adoption or when smaller political parties actually adopt a quota, there is a potential electoral cost to the party, government, or even specific elite for not responding to this pressure. And, on the other hand, there is a potential benefit as well: if the party adopts a gender quota after social movement activism or after its supporters request it, the party or individual elite will be seen as responsive to the demands of their constituents.

It is critical to emphasize, however, that the potential cost or benefit of responding to the demands of constituents or activists is not constant across systems or even across parties in the same system. Instead, the cost or benefit of responsiveness hinges strongly on both the cultural acceptance of women's equality as well as the particular ideological position of the political party, government, or individual elite. For example, if the party is on the left wing of the ideological spectrum, then being responsive to calls for increased equality will more likely be a benefit than a cost. If, however, the party is on the ideological right wing, then responding to activist calls for a gender quota could actually alienate constituents and undermine the electoral success of the party. This does not necessarily mean that all left-wing parties will be supportive of women's social movements (as noted by Beckwith [2000], left-wing parties have a mixed record of responding to feminist movements), but rather that the elite's calculation of whether or not to be responsive is impacted by the ideological position of the party. Further, McCammon et al. (2001) emphasize the importance of cultural attitudes about women's roles in society on determining the success of women's social movements for suffrage, and this finding is applicable to women's inclusion at the elite level as well. In those states where cultural norms about women's traditional role in the home have modernized, the benefit for being responsive to calls for inclusion is much greater than in those where the majority of citizens continue to support traditional gender roles.

THE INTERNATIONAL RESPONSIVENESS COST OR BENEFIT

The international realm—in which I include international organizations such as the United Nations (UN) and European Union (EU) as well as international non-governmental organizations (NGOs) such as the Women's Environment and Development Organization—also generates a cost or benefit in the calculation of women's potential inclusion. The nature of this variable depends strongly on the relationship between the particular state and the specific international entity; some states may view women's increased inclusion as a path to increasing much-needed foreign aid, while others may see following an IO's suggested policies of inclusion as sending a signal of commitment to rules and norms of the organization, thereby increasing the likelihood of trust and long-term involvement between the country and IO. Thus, as is the case for the other variables, the impact of the international realm is context specific; one cannot assume that states will automatically follow the requests and suggestions of international actors regarding gender equality.

For those countries dependent on foreign aid, women's increased inclusion carries a substantial potential benefit. That is, because women are associated with democracy (an idea I expand upon in chapter 3), those countries seeking foreign aid can adopt policies that advance women's political participation (such as gender quotas) and expect an increase in foreign aid to follow (Bush 2011; Paxton and Hughes 2017). Further, Bush (2015) finds that, in addition to the recipient countries themselves, the NGOs that facilitate foreign aid tend to prefer democracy assistance programs that offer support for women's political participation because they are "measurable and regime-compatible" (p. 14). Gender quotas, for example, are "regime-compatible" because, unlike changes in freedom of the press or increased protection of dissidents, adding gender quotas does not pose any threat to the regime, and thus NGOs do not have to be concerned that their support of this policy with endanger their future in the recipient country. However, while foreign aid is a potential benefit, it is important to note that the power of this potential benefit depends in large part on how dependent the country is on foreign aid and thus, is not always in the elite calculus of inclusion.

For those countries not dependent on foreign aid, the potential international realm benefit or cost of women's inclusion is different and arguably more complex. These countries—typically advanced democracies—are more concerned with developing long-term and mutually beneficial relationships with IOs than with immediate tangible benefits such as aid. Thus, when the EU or UN recommends the increased inclusion of women, a potential benefit to following that recommendation is that it signals that the country is committed to the IO; it is, therefore, not necessarily the case that the country is concerned about advancing women's equality, but rather that, depending on the other variables in the inclusion calculation, following the equality directive of the IO may be the least costly method of signaling commitment to the IO. For example, Van der Vleuten (2007) offers an analysis of EU gender policies and finds that, particularly in the past two decades, "governments saw the implementation of new social policies as a way of building support for European integration and the single currency" (p. 147). And further, because certain gender-equity policies are more costly than others—instituting paid parental leave, for example, is economically costly to the state that adopts that policy—following the recommendations for increasing the presence of women in politics is actually a lower cost method of signaling support. Again, this benefit does not necessarily mean an increase in women's inclusion will occur—that depends on the other variables in the inclusion calculation as well—but rather that women's presence in the domestic government has the potential to be beneficial to elites who want to signal support for an international norm or entity.

However, if the government does follow the recommendations of an IO, there is the potential for an international responsiveness cost to result. This cost refers to domestic voter backlash against the action taken in favor of equality and, similar to the domestic responsiveness cost, is more of an issue for those governments made up of political parties that support traditional gender roles. For example, as Baldez (2014) explains in her analysis of why the United States has not ratified the UN's CEDAW Treaty,[3] the deeply partisan nature of gender equality in the United States means that the modern Republican party faces a relatively high cost of ratification. Thus, because of this potential domestic backlash by Republican voters, the cost of being responsive to the international realm may, for elites in that party, outweigh the benefits of women's potential inclusion.

TIP THE BALANCE: THE INFLUENCE OF WOMEN IN PROXIMITY

While a foundational assumption of this book is that the rational opportunists who determine women's access to power are male, it is important to consider women's influence on those men, as well as the reality that there are some women in positions of real power. As I discuss in chapter 1, the presence and power of those women is very limited and existing literature has under-stated the continuing power of the patriarchy over the positions women are able to reach and what they are able to do. But nevertheless, while not ruling unilaterally, women are now at least "in the room where it happens." What influence do they have over the inclusion decision of the male rational opportunist?

Some of the existing literature on the effect of women in party leadership has found a powerful relationship between women's presence at the elite level and their inclusion as candidates: the more women in party leadership, the more likely that women candidates are selected (Caul 1999; Kunovich and Paxton 2005; Cheng and Tavits 2011, though see also Tremblay and Pelletier 2001). And, while there is little systematic research on the effect of wives, daughters, or mothers on the decision-making process of male elites, the anecdote of Abigail Adams urging her husband to "remember the ladies" illustrates the potential of even spouses to draw attention to the importance of women's inclusion.

However, while we know that women's presence in the environment *can* matter, there is little scholarly consensus on exactly what the mechanism is here. Cheng and Tavits (2011) offer three possible explanations for this correlation between the presence of women elites and the inclusion of more women candidates. First, it could be because, just like the men, women elites feel less threatened when surrounded by people like themselves and thus are predisposed to want to increase the presence of women. Second, women elites tend to be in professional networks that include other women, and thus it is likely that they are familiar with qualified women they can easily recruit. Third is the "indirect signaling effect" of women's presence in the elite (p. 462): for women outside of the political elite, seeing women in power is a signal that it is acceptable for women to be active in politics and thus increases the likelihood that they run for office.

In addition to the possible explanations outlined by Cheng and Tavits (2011), another common—and sometimes implicit—argument found in existing literature on women's descriptive representation is that women in power exert pressure on the male elites by threatening to expose them as sexist if they do not increase women's presence in office. For example, in her analysis of the adoption of a gender quota in Mexico, Baldez (2004) explains that "cross-partisan coalitions of female politicians who can credibly *threaten* to denounce their male colleagues as sexist for opposing quotas represent a powerful pro-quota force" (p. 234, my emphasis). Thus, the literature on the adoption of gender quotas, in particular, argues that the presence of women in power could lead to the inclusion of more women because of their potential to activate constituent awareness and thereby create a domestic responsiveness benefit.

However, while all of these explanations are plausible and undoubtedly true in certain contexts, the causal reasoning of why and how the presence of women in power sometimes leads to the inclusion of more women is still shrouded in mystery. In short, we just don't know why this is happening and, while the explanations presented here are plausible, none of them are without fault. And this is a problem because, without an understanding of the mechanism, scholars cannot gauge the conditions that will strengthen or weaken this effect. For example, it is reasonable to expect the "indirect signaling effect" in certain circumstances, but there is also reason to believe that, under other circumstances, women's presence in office will signal aspiring women that society has not yet accepted their leadership and thus it is best to stay away. That is, when women leaders are threatened with physical violence, harassed online, and/or just generally treated with disdain by misogynists in society, this decreases the likelihood that women will want to run for office. Krook (2017) explains that:

Sexist hostility and intimidation have driven female politicians out of politics. . . . young women appear to internalize these lessons in ways that reduce their own political ambitions. In Australia, 60 percent of women aged 18 to 21 and 80 percent of those over 31 said that they were less likely to run for office after misogynistic attacks against Prime Minister Julia Gillard. Nearly all participants in a program for aspiring women leaders in the United Kingdom stated that they had witnessed sexist abuse of female politicians online, and over 75 percent said that it weighed on their decision about whether to seek a role in public life. (p. 84)

This mechanism, therefore, will only work under certain conditions, and thus, perhaps the overarching relationship between women elites and the increased inclusion of women will also only hold under certain conditions.

Further, another problem with the common explanations for this relationship is that they all tend to rest on the faulty premise that women elites will *want* to increase the presence of other women in power. And yet this does not seem accurate. Just like the men, women are rational opportunists; it is false to assume that women, perhaps due to their stereotyped communal traits, are more likely to facilitate the inclusion of other women even if it doesn't benefit them or their party (Rudman and Glick 2001). Further, it is crucial to note that those women who have achieved some sort of influence or limited access to power are still fully immersed in the patriarchy, which will be reflected in their own cost/benefit calculation of women's inclusion. For example, existing research on how women behave in senior leadership positions suggests that, in order to maintain their own power and survival, some women leaders in primarily male organizations tend to reproduce the gender hierarchy rather than undermine it (Ellemers et al. 2012; Derks et al. 2016). Particularly in settings where women are devalued or negatively stereotyped, senior women behave so as "to assimilate into male-dominated organizations in which men are valued over women . . . their reluctance to help other women to achieve similar career success is a consequence of this assimilation strategy" (Derks et al. 2016, p. 458). It is not that women are more competitive with women, but rather that their success in a patriarchal environment can depend, in part, on their willingness to maintain the patriarchy.

Finally, even if women in the elite do want to increase the presence of women candidates, it is critically important to not overstate their ability to unilaterally implement this desire. There are two reasons to expect that women may be constrained in their ability to increase the presence of other women: first, as Norris and Lovenduski (1993) note, women party leaders, just like the men, are constrained by the institutions of their party and country. For example, if candidate nomination occurs at the local level or via primary elections, national-level elites have a more difficult time controlling candidate selection, no matter their gender. And second, as discussed in chapter 1, the number of women party elites is limited, and none of them have unilateral power. Thus, it is unreasonable to expect them to be able to exert their will if the other rational opportunists in leadership do not see a benefit to women's inclusion. That being said, women elites could use their power and access to generate a domestic or international demand for more women in office—that is, to trigger a domestic or international responsiveness benefit—which may, in turn, alter the inclusion calculation. Additionally, one could see women's presence in the elite as being particularly impactful under conditions of uncertainty. If, for example, the rational opportunist is uncertain about the threat cost of adopting a gender quota, then women in the environment could influence that perception of threat and potentially change it. Thus, it seems most realistic to anticipate that women's elite presence has a potential indirect effect on women's inclusion through their ability to generate domestic or international benefits, but that this effect is not direct, unilateral, or guaranteed.

There is no easy answer here to the question of women's influence; it is difficult to know for sure exactly why women in leadership positions are sometimes willing and able to open the doors to more women, and sometimes not. Thus, rather than adding this concept as an additional variable in the inclusion calculation, I refer to the effect of women in the elite as tipping the balance. Because of the lack of certainty as to how and why this relationship between women elites and women's inclusion works, one cannot anticipate under what conditions this relationship occurs and what factors exacerbate or weaken it. It may matter sometimes, but not always, and scholars are not yet sure as to exactly when this variable makes a difference. Thus, it is difficult to map and predict the effects of women's elite presence in the inclusion calculation. And yet, I am not prepared to dismiss it entirely from consideration, as there is evidence that women's elite presence has a correlation with women's inclusion, and further, it makes logical sense that this presence would matter under certain conditions. This variable therefore remains outside of the core inclusion calculation of the rational opportunist but should not be conceived of as unimportant in women's inclusion.

A BREAK IN THE STATUS QUO: THE EFFECT
OF CHANGING CONDITIONS

While one cannot use the decision-making calculus described above to generate a perfect prediction of elite behavior, the limited number of women in politics suggests a relatively clear trend: in the mind of the rational opportunist, the costs of women's inclusion usually outweigh the benefits. That is, as I have described them, the potential threat, displacement, and incongruity costs are substantial (though they do vary), and the benefits from domestic or international responsiveness are potentially significant yet mediated by several factors (e.g., the ideological orientation of the party in question, the prevalence of social movements, and the country's position in the international realm). Further, the limited presence of women in elite positions, while important, does not have a dramatic impact on the calculation. Thus, it seems that, under most circumstances, the male rational opportunist will decide that there are more costs than benefits associated with increasing women's inclusion.

However, when one drops the assumption of status quo political conditions, the inclusion calculation changes. That is, the conceptualization of the inclusion calculation has thus far assumed status quo conditions in which there is relative social, political, and institutional stability. This is the norm for many elections, but it is not entirely unusual for an election to occur under conditions of change or upheaval. The existing literature on the effect of crisis on women's descriptive representation is limited, but there are important exceptions: Saint-Germain (1993) notes the role of crisis in undermining traditional gender roles, thereby making women's presence in the political sphere more palatable to citizens. Hughes (2009) offers a path-breaking analysis of women's representation in the post-civil-war environment and presents several possible structural, political, and cultural mechanisms that could be responsible for the post-war increases in women's inclusion. In general, these mechanisms highlight the increased opportunities for women due to the political system overhaul that typically follows civil war (a lower displacement cost) as well as the power of changing gender norms (a lower incongruity cost) and the benefit of using women's representation as a way to attract international monetary support (a higher international responsiveness benefit). Finally, there is a line of literature that engages the "think crisis-think female" phenomena, in which the context of threat or crisis increases peoples' preference for women leaders due to their stereotypical association with change (Brown et al. 2011) or their stereotypical association with traits that are useful for managing people in a crisis situation (Ryan et al. 2010).

Thus, it seems that a break in the status quo triggers a break in the typical characteristics that voters are looking for in their leaders, which in turn transforms at least part of the incongruity cost into a potential benefit. This break in the status quo is not necessarily dramatic—it does not have to be war—it can also encompass slower transformations that undermine the legitimacy of the government or political party. In this environment, the stereotypes associated with women increase in value and thus, in these particular settings, the rational opportunist should view women's presence as more valuable as well. Her stereotypes, I argue, will not just affect her own fortunes, but also the party as a whole; her presence becomes a signal that the institution she is associated with is feminizing. However, this potential gain is temporary; the incongruity cost reverts back to full strength when the period of change is complete.

Existing literature on the dynamic value and use of stereotypes focuses primarily on the conditions under which masculine stereotypes become more valuable. For example, the scholarly consensus is that voters are more likely to seek out male candidates during times of war or terrorist threat due to the stereotypes of men as more aggressive, strong, and protective (Lawless 2004; Falk and Kenski 2006; Holman et al. 2016). The mechanism argued for is the power of priming, which is defined as a psychological tendency for people to focus more on the information that is being emphasized rather than examine the entire informational landscape equally (Kahneman et al. 1982; Iyengar and Kinder 1987; Krosnick and Kinder 1990). As Krosnick and Kinder (1990) explain, "people tend to forgo such exhaustive analyses and instead employ intuitive shortcuts and simple rules of thumb. One such heuristic is to rely upon information that is most accessible in memory" (p. 499). Thus, when there is a terrorist threat, and especially one that the media is covering extensively, voters are "primed" to focus on that threat of violence more than other factors and, in turn, "individuals come to place even more value on traits and capabilities that are stereotypically masculine" (Holman et al. 2016, p. 138).

If priming increases the value of masculine traits in the context of war, then there must also be environments in which voters are primed to place more value on stereotypically feminine traits. I suggest that there are at least two political contexts in which the traits associated with women increase in value: first, when a massive government corruption scandal is revealed; second, when a hybrid regime takes steps away from democratic principles by either reducing civil rights or changing electoral law to unfairly favor the sitting regime. In these contexts, the government and/or political party are losing legitimacy due to a public perception that they are corrupt, greedy, or subverting the rules of democracy. And thus, the stereotypical personality traits associated with women gain value; this is the moment when citizens are looking for evidence that the greed and malfeasance will soon end and be replaced with inclusion, stability, and honesty. And thus, I argue that in both of these contexts, women's bodies can be utilized as symbols of characteristics that are not typically associated with government; women's traits are no longer incongruent with good leadership in these environments, but instead are viewed as a useful signal that whatever problem has created the crisis or change will end. This does not automatically mean that political parties will run more women or that governments will all rush to associate themselves with women; rather, it means that a previous cost associated with women's inclusion partially transitions to a benefit. Thus, in these particular political contexts, women candidates increase in value, which may tip the balance in the elite calculation of their inclusion.

CONCLUSION

In this chapter, I presented a new conceptualization of the process of women's inclusion by grounding the current literature in a frame of elite rationality. While existing literature does not explicitly engage this frame, scholars' current understanding of the factors that impact women's descriptive representation fit well into a schema of calculation; it seems likely that the costs and benefits of women's inclusion are more likely driving descriptive representation than the angelic or demonic tendencies of party elites. Thus, I presented the factors that are recognized in the literature as having a significant impact on descriptive representation as costs and benefits in an overall elite calculation of women's inclusion.

In addition, I offered a new perspective on the issue of incongruity. Under conditions of change or chaos, citizens not only update their beliefs on women's roles but also temporarily change their understanding of the ideal leader. This brings new value to the stereotypes traditionally associated with women which, I argue, increases the value of women's inclusion in the eyes of the elite. This perspective is in opposition to the common yet usually implicit belief that under conditions of chaos or massive change, the doors of power are left unguarded, allowing women to rush in grab power. Instead, I portray chaos as changing the calculation of women's inclusion; even in the most dire of circumstances, party elites do not throw open the access to positions of power, nor do they wander away from those doors, allowing women to slip in. Instead, one should conceptualize the post-crisis political environment as remarkably similar to the pre-crisis political environment: it is patriarchal and consists of rational opportunists attempting to maintain their hold on power. What changes, therefore, are the costs and benefits of women's inclusion; placing women on the ballot or adopting a gender quota is a simple way for party elites to give the impression of a shift toward honesty or democratization without having to do any of the difficult work of fundamental reform.

In the following chapter, I focus on one variable in the inclusion calculation—the incongruity benefit—and provide a deeper analysis of the mechanism that underlies it. I begin with a detailed discussion of the literature on stereotypes associated with women and then present the results of an original survey on traits associated with women leaders in Canada and the United States. Both the existing literature as well as the survey results suggest that while traditional feminine stereotypes continue to be powerful, some people view these stereotypical traits as potentially valuable in government. I then expand on the logic of the incongruity benefit, and suggest that male elites see a benefit to "feminization by association" under some conditions. In other words, because of the power of gender stereotypes, citizens view women's presence as a signal about the institutions in which they participate which, in turn, can potentially increase the value of women's inclusion in the eyes of male elites.

Feminine Stereotypes and
the Advantages of Association

INTRODUCTION

Women's roles in society have changed in dramatic ways over the past century, yet many traditional gender stereotypes are holding strong. Even with more and more examples of women starting wars, getting caught in corruption schemes, and just generally behaving like stereotypical male politicians, the assumptions that women are "naturally" more maternal, cooperative, and honest than men are not fading. What has changed, however, is the general objection to women in politics; in most countries, it is now rare for the average citizen to believe that women have no place in the public sphere under any circumstances. And thus, now that this automatic rejection of women in politics is no longer the norm, women candidates and legislators have a potential new value to elites. These stereotypes associated with women—which were used for a long time to keep them out of politics—are no longer viewed as antithetical to politics but instead as potentially valuable under certain conditions. In other words, traditional feminine traits are potentially useful to both women's electoral fortunes and the political parties or governments with which they are associated.

This chapter focuses on one variable in the inclusion calculation: the incongruity benefit. I begin by discussing the feminine stereotypes that are the foundation of this benefit, paying particular attention to those that are potentially most useful to male elites: the assumptions that women in politics are more honest and committed to democracy than men. I offer examples of these stereotypes being employed as justifications for state and NGO actions and argue that the frequent use of these stereotypes as justifications demonstrates their power in the minds of citizens. In addition, I present the results of an original survey of citizens in the United States and Canada, which suggests that while most citizens continue to value men over women as leaders, they do see women as potentially bringing valuable traits to the political realm. I then expand on my central argument underlying the mechanism of the incongruity benefit, explaining that because of their assumed personality traits, associating the party or government with women can be valuable. Women are not interpreted simply as neutral representatives of their district or party but are also thought of as more honest, different from the norm, and as an overall symbol of democracy. Thus, male elites can strategically increase the presence of women legislators to give citizens the impression of a new embrace of honesty or even democracy, even though those elites may have no sincere interest in increasing women's power.

STEREOTYPES: THE ASSOCIATION OF WOMEN WITH COMMUNAL PERSONALITY TRAITS

Even as the roles of women in society change and grow, traditional gender stereotypes continue to be surprisingly powerful and enduring. This may be because of how early they become ingrained in our psyches: children begin to associate certain personality traits or behaviors on the basis of gender before they can even walk and then continue to build on the stereotypes throughout their early years (Serbin et al. 2001; Zosuls et al. 2009). And as adults, even those who have consciously attempted to sever their attachment to traditional stereotypes continue to be impacted by them due to the power of "implicit bias." This type of bias exists without the knowledge or consent of its holder and thus can "bypass conscious processes that might otherwise serve as a defense against sexism" (Rudman et al.

2001, p. 1164). Implicit biases are, therefore, in the words of Greenwald and Krieger (2006), "especially intriguing, and also especially problematic, because they can produce behavior that diverges from a person's avowed or endorsed beliefs or principles" (p. 951). In other words, the conscious mind may be in direct conflict with the biases and yet affected by their power nonetheless. Further, unlike more explicit forms of bias, time does not appear to reduce the power of implicit bias; recent and on-going research on implicit bias from Banaji and Greenwald (2016) suggests that these "hidden biases" continue to have a strong impact on our judgement of and behavior toward members of particular social groups.

When people make assumptions about the personality traits of a person based on her gender, the most common stereotype they engage is that a woman has more "communal" qualities than a man (Bem 1981; Alexander and Anderson 1993; Huddy and Terkildsen 1993; Spence and Buckner 2000; Eagly and Karau 2002; Sanbonmatsu 2002). Communal traits are those associated with traditional notions of femininity, such as being compassionate, sensitive, cooperative, gentle, honest, and loyal. These are, in short, attributes that one associates with an idealized vision of a mother; it is the assumption that when one identifies as woman, one is also inherently a caretaker who is fundamentally concerned with the well-being of others. It is important to emphasize that this stereotype is not limited to the United States; scholarship has demonstrated that, while there is variability in the specific stereotypes associated with women depending on country and/or cultural identification, there is also a strong association between women and communal traits around the world (Williams and Best 1990; Glick et al. 2000).

These commonly held stereotypes illustrate the fact that many of the personality traits associated with women today are prima facie positive. Prejudice against the abilities or presence of women, therefore, is not necessarily drawn from a negative or hateful predisposition about women. This does not mean that hateful gender stereotypes do not exist or even that these prima facie positive stereotypes do not trigger negative consequences (i.e., the incongruity cost continues to exist), but rather that there are many stereotypes associated with women that fall under the

"women are wonderful" designation coined by Eagly and Mladinic (1994). Also known as "benevolent sexism," this type of prejudice causes the believer to see women as inherently good, pure, and kind, and thus requiring that they be cherished and protected as special (Glick and Fiske 1996).

In existing analyses of political behavior, there is substantial evidence that stereotypes from the "women are wonderful" category are frequently engaged by citizens. Specifically, the stereotype that women are more honest, naïve, and uninterested in the deceit and corruption often associated with politics has been demonstrated to play an important role in the voter calculus in several different scenarios (Alexander and Andersen 1993; Shames 2003). For example, McDermott (1998) demonstrates a significant correlation between the likelihood of choosing a female candidate and concern for ethics: in her quasi-experiment of telephone interviews, those respondents who felt that "ethics in government" was one of the most important problems in California were more likely to prefer the hypothetical woman candidate for governor. Baldez (2002) provides another example of this stereotype in action through her discussion of women's groups in Chile. She finds that even though many women were active in political parties, they used a strategy of claiming to be non-partisan political outsiders so as to mobilize voters against the parties in the opposition. Because the voters did indeed assume that the women were political outsiders, this political strategy proved to be quite effective.

In addition, there is substantial evidence that governments and international organizations view the association of women with honesty and integrity as accurate and powerful enough to be a part of policy decisions. Goetz (2007), for example, highlights Peru's attempt to end corruption in their police force by transferring all jobs in the traffic division to women and Mexico's decision to staff its customs service "anti-corruption force" with only women officers. She also notes similar behavior in Uganda, where the bureaucratic positions of treasurer in local governments across the country are disproportionately assigned to women. International organizations have promoted this association as well. *The National Democratic Institute*—a non-profit with an explicit goal of promoting and maintaining democracy—states on their website that it is essential to include women in developing democracies because "women are particularly effective in promoting honest government." [1] Another example is found on the doors of the public entrance of the UN headquarters in New York City: four sculpted metal pictures depict the virtues espoused by the organization, and the symbols of peace, justice, and truth are represented by women (figs. 3.1 and 3.2).[2]

Perhaps due to the prevalent stereotypes of women as honest, cooperative, and generally maternal, there is also a powerful association of women with democracy. This association is not new—the ancient Romans declared Libertas the goddess of freedom and liberty. And in 1792, the French decided that their official seal would feature a woman—Marianne—who would represent liberty and republicanism. She was briefly removed from all government materials during Napoleon's reign (he, of course, replaced her with his own image) but returned after the revolution and is now

Figures 3.1 and 3.2 Depictions of Justice and Truth at UN Headquarters
SOURCE: Author photograph.

found on French currency, government documents, and stamps.[3] Perhaps
one of the most famous representations of this symbolism of women is
found in the painting *La Liberté Guidant le Peuple*, in which a woman,
personifying freedom and democracy, steps over dead bodies, raising the
French flag in an inspiring way (fig. 3.3).

In recent years, the association of women with democracy has gained in
popularity, and the symbolism is no longer isolated to western countries.
During the Tiananmen Square uprising in China in 1989, for example, the
protesters assembled a 33-foot tall statue of a woman holding a torch and
named her the "Spirit of Democracy." This was not simply a copy of the
United States' Statue of Liberty; it was, in the words of one protester, "the
soul of the 1989 Chinese democracy movement."[4]

The association of women with democracy is not false; it is indeed the
case, as Phillips (1995) noted, that the inclusion of women in government

Figure 3.3 *La Liberté Guidant le Peuple* by Eugène Delacroix.
SOURCE: Wikimedia Commons.

is a basic and necessary element of a democracy. But the idea that a democracy *should* include women in government has shifted in recent years and is now more commonly referenced as its transformed *if/then* version. That is, the association between women and democracy has transformed to be prescriptive: *if* women are included in government, *then* the democracy will be more healthy or successful. In a 2016 policy paper published by the Carnegie Endowment for International Peace, Carothers (2016) asserts that:

> acceptance has grown of the general principle that women's political equality is central to the quality and integrity of democratic practice and governance. The idea that women's political empowerment contributes directly to, and in some ways is a prerequisite for, sustainable development also has gained ground. (P. 4)

Perhaps even more telling, the policy paper itself is titled "Democracy Support Strategies: Leading with Women's Political Empowerment." And this is not a unique perspective: a World Bank research report from 2001 advocates for an increased number of women in government because "increasing women's voice in politics and public life can improve the impact of policies and programs, reduce corruption, and strengthen governance" (King and Mason 2001, p. 268). And further, the National Democratic Institute (NDI) explicitly declares women's increased political participation as a prerequisite for a healthy democracy, stating that: "NDI believes that equitable participation of women in politics and government is essential to building and sustaining democracy."[5]

Bush (2011) also notes the association of women and democracy in her discussion of the adoption of gender quotas. She explains that there is a "democracy establishment" in the international realm, which is a network of intergovernmental, governmental, and nongovernmental actors, and that these governments and organizations "share a common set of normative *cause-effect* beliefs" (p. 111, my emphasis). One of the core beliefs of this network is that the presence of women in a state is fundamental to a successful democratic transition, and thus developing regimes now adopt gender quotas as a signal that their regime is transitioning to be more democratic. Thus, no matter their political stance or beliefs about the regime, women's mere presence is now interpreted as a sign of democracy.

Therefore, it is clear that the already complicated relationship between gender stereotypes and conceptions of good leadership has become even more complex in the twenty-first century. Rather than a simple story of overt misogyny, there are now some stereotypes that help women's electoral fortunes. But there also continues to be evidence of a strong incongruency in the minds of voters about women and leadership and thus, because of these conflicting expectations, it can be difficult to develop a systematic theory for how voters respond to women candidates. In an effort to better understand how modern voters view the role and value of feminine stereotypes in leadership, the next section offers the results of an original survey on stereotypes and leadership.

SURVEY: GENDER STEREOTYPES AND LEADERSHIP IN THE TWENTY-FIRST CENTURY

While I argue that women have gained a new symbolic value in recent years, thus far I have only presented secondary evidence to support this claim. In this section, I offer the results of an original survey on gender stereotypes and leadership, with the goal of establishing both the assumptions that citizens make about women legislators as well as the potential value of these assumptions to party or government elites. This survey was performed in the pacific northwest of the United States and Canada, with the subject population consisting of the following groups: graduate and undergraduate students at three universities on the west coast of the United States; undergraduate students at one university in Canada; and non-students at Leupold and Stevens, Inc., a gun-scope manufacturing company.[6] The decision to perform the survey at Leupold and Stevens as well as at universities with vastly different student profiles was made in an effort to increase the external validity of the results.[7] While the majority of the participants were students, a comparison of the results from the non-student group at

Leopold and Stevens with those of students demonstrated no significant variation; that is, both students and non-students responded to the survey in similar ways, thereby providing evidence that these results are generalizable beyond students.[8] Participants were compensated with candy bars, doughnuts, or extra credit; no financial compensation was given for their time. This is clearly not a random sample, but as table 3.1 illustrates, it does provide at least some demographic variation.

The format of the survey was as follows: after the participant finished a simulated voting exercise, he/she was given the survey. The first substantive section of the survey focused on establishing the respondent's opinions on both the least and most desired personality traits of legislators—at this point, no reference to gender was made. Based on the list of personality traits created by Williams and Best (1990), I provided a list of 66 traits: 41 were selected because they were, according to Williams and Best, *not* overwhelmingly associated with one gender or another. The other 25 traits were selected precisely because Williams and Best found them to be strongly associated with one gender but not the other. For example, the term "whiny" is overwhelmingly associated with women, and the term "arrogant" is overwhelmingly associated with men. The chosen 66 traits were divided into two sections in the survey. The first, "positive" section, included 30 traits and asked respondents, "How important is it that a legislator have this trait?" The second, "negative" section, included 36 traits and asked, "How important is it that a legislator *not* have this trait?" In both sections, participants responded by checking a box next to the following categories: very important, important, somewhat important, and not important at all.[9]

Table 3.2 presents those traits marked by more than 50% of participants as "very important" for their legislators to either have or not have. In other words, these are the most and least desirable traits in legislators. The potential power associated with honesty is clear: almost 82% of participants declared it to be essential to a legislator, and 81% declared dishonesty an objectionable trait. However, while there are some words that are traditionally associated with women (e.g., whiny) and some traditionally associated with men (e.g., reckless) in these results, one cannot determine the

Table 3.1 DEMOGRAPHIC BREAKDOWN OF SURVEY PARTICIPANTS

	Raw Number of Participants	Percentage (%)
SURVEY LOCATION		
United States	356	66.7
Canada	178	33.3
GENDER		
Male	272	50.9
Female	262	49.1
AGE		
18-22	360	67.3
23-27	80	15.0
Over 28	95	17.8
STUDENT MAJOR		
Political Science	161	32.1
Undecided/Undeclared	37	7.4
CCJ (Criminology And Criminal Justice)	31	6.2
Sociology	24	4.8
Community Development	22	4.4
Other	227	45.2
BIRTHPLACE		
United States	328	61.7
California	62	18.9
Oregon	166	50.6
Washington	25	7.6
Other States	75	22.9
INTERNATIONAL	204	38.3
Canada	96	47.1
China	15	7.4
South Korea	14	6.9
Hong Kong	8	3.9
Other	71	34.8
IDEOLOGY—PARTICIPANTS IN CANADA		
Conservative Party	34	20.6
Liberal Party	91	55.2

Table 3.1 CONTINUED

	Raw Number of Participants	Percentage (%)
New Democratic Party	34	20.6
Green Party	6	3.6
IDEOLOGY—PARTICIPANTS IN THE UNITED STATES		
Democrat	152	45.1
Neither (but prefer Democrat or Republican)	128	38.0
Republican	57	16.9

Table 3.2 MOST AND LEAST DESIRABLE TRAITS ASSOCIATED WITH LEGISLATORS

Traits of Legislators	Percentage of Participants (%)
LEAST DESIRABLE	
Dishonest	81.33
Careless	78.19
Greedy	68.21
Absent Minded	65.43
Cowardly	59.89
Reckless	59.70
Intolerant	59.52
Weak	56.75
Whiny	54.16
MOST DESIRABLE	
Intelligent	86.32
Honest	81.89
Rational	73.57
Logical	71.16
Confident	59.15

NOTE: Only those traits that more than 50% of participants marked as "very important" for their legislators to have or not to have are presented here.

strategic value of women legislators without establishing the stereotypes associated with each gender. Thus, in section two of the survey, I explicitly focus on the stereotypes associated with male and female legislators. In this section, I offer the respondent the opportunity to select 3 adjectives that typically describe female legislators from the trait lists of 66 positive and negative attributes and then to select 3 adjectives from the same lists that typically describe male legislators. In table 3.3, I present those adjectives that more than 5% of respondents associated with either male or female legislators.

These results provide several insights into the modern manifestation of gender bias: first, there is obvious evidence that the traditional stereotypes about men and women continue to exist: "aggressive" and "strong" were the top two traits named by participants to describe male leaders, while traditional feminine norms such as "sensitive," "tolerant," and "pacifying" were listed in the top five most common descriptors for women leaders. Participants, in short, continue to believe that men and women legislators are innately different, and that they are different in traditional ways. However, looking back at table 3.2, these traditionally feminine traits were not named as least desirable traits by a majority of respondents, which offers some evidence that traditional feminine traits associated with women are no longer viewed as incompatible with leadership. Second, the trait named as the most desirable for legislators to have—intelligence—is most strongly associated with women: 12.94% of respondents named it as one of their three characteristics that best describes a typical female legislator, while 7% named it as a descriptor of a typical male legislator. Finally, the association of women with honesty is supported by these results. While only 6% of respondents specifically listed honesty as one of the three traits that they associate with women legislators, 9% wrote the word "sincere," a synonym of honesty, to describe women. Respondents did not use the words "sincere" or "honest" when describing typical male legislators, instead listing words that suggested a perception of men as more likely to sacrifice honesty for personal gain. For example, 11% of respondents wrote the word "greedy" as one of their three descriptors of male legislators, and 11% wrote the word "opportunistic." In addition, 5.47% of respondents

Table 3.3 TRAITS ASSOCIATED WITH MEN VERSUS WOMEN LEGISLATORS

Traits	Percentage of Participants (%)
MOST ASSOCIATED WITH WOMEN LEGISLATORS	
Sensitive	15.92
Intelligent	12.94
Ambitious	11.44
Tolerant	10.95
Pacifying/Peace-Making	9.95
Sincere	8.96
Rational	8.46
Cautious	7.46
Gentle	7.46
Stubborn	7.46
Moody	6.47
Submissive	6.47
Confident	5.97
Honest	5.97
Aggressive	5.47
Outspoken	5.47
Patient	5.47
MOST ASSOCIATED WITH MEN LEGISLATORS	
Aggressive	28.86
Strong	19.90
Confident	18.41
Stubborn	17.91
Ambitious	14.93
Arrogant	12.94
Outspoken	11.44
Greedy	10.95
Opportunistic	10.95
Logical	8.96
Egotistical	8.46

(*continued*)

Table 3.3 CONTINUED

Traits	Percentage of Participants (%)
Loud	7.46
Forceful	6.97
Intelligent	6.97
Rational	6.97
Rude	6.97
Dishonest	5.47

offered the word "dishonest" to describe male legislators. None of those words were used by more than 5% of respondents to describe women.

From the looks of these results, one might be tempted to declare that, in the eyes of the voters, men and women legislators are now equally valued. But I caution you to resist that urge for several reasons. First, the effect of social desirability pressures might have caused survey respondents to misrepresent their beliefs about women legislators. As Streb et al. (2007) and Krupnikov et al. (2016) noted, it can be difficult to accurately track voter reactions to women candidates due to the embarrassment associated with blatant prejudice. Thus, surveys and experiments that give a respondent the opportunity to voice prejudiced beliefs (such as this one) under-report the level of prejudice actually felt by the respondents. Second, even with the pressure to avoid appearing prejudiced, an interesting phenomenon occurred that suggests an undercurrent of backlash against women leaders just beneath the surface: Of the 35 participants who did not follow the instructions of the survey to select their three descriptors from the provided list of 66 adjectives, 3 of them wrote words that are synonymous with a rejection of women's power. In other words, 35 participants got creative and named words or offered phrases that were not on the list of adjectives and, of these 35 rogue participants, two of them wrote the word "bitch" to describe women legislators, and one wrote the word "butch." The off-book traits used to describe male legislators were much less dramatic, with perhaps the most interesting being that men "speak before thinking." This is, of course, just a small group of people and thus one wouldn't want to overstate the meaning of this unexpected outcome. However, it would be improper to err in the other direction as well—the fact that three people (nearly 10% of the rogue participants) were comfortable enough with their misogyny to actually write the word "bitch" or "butch" on a survey should not be ignored. This result suggests that the "backlash effect" first noted by Rudman (1998) continues to be an issue.

In addition to the surprising behaviors of the rogue respondents, another result of the survey suggests that there continues to be an underlying preference for traits traditionally associated with men. As demonstrated in table 3.2, "confidence" was named as a most desirable trait of legislators by nearly 60% of the respondents. Further, almost 60% ranked being "cowardly" as a least desirable trait, and 57% ranked being "weak" as least desirable. As table 3.3 reveals, confidence is overwhelmingly associated with men (18.41% of respondents wrote it down as a typical trait of a male legislator). And, while the words "weak" or "cowardly" were not used to describe women by more than 5% of respondents, its antonyms, the words "strong" and "aggressive," were the most common words listed to describe men. Finally, while intelligence is, according to these results, more associated with women than men, none of the traditionally feminine traits—other than honesty—were named as most desired characteristics of legislators. In other words, the traditional communal traits associated with the mothering ideal—such as, sensitive, pacifying, cautious, gentle—were not ranked as very important for legislators to possess. And, if one reads "weak" or "cowardly" as negative interpretations of communal stereotypes, then there seems to be a systematic reaction against traditional female traits in leaders. These results suggest, therefore, that while some feminine traits are viewed as valuable, the pendulum has not swung in the other direction; traits traditionally associated with men continue to be the most valued and accepted as the norm of good leadership.

In sum, it seems that both the original survey and existing literature suggest that, while women and men leaders are not viewed as interchangeable, citizens believe that women have the potential to bring valuable traits to the leadership realm. Thus, one can conclude that blatant misogyny has lessened; being female is no longer viewed as an unacceptable characteristic in an office-seeker. Instead, a typical response of modern citizens is to view women as offering personality traits that, especially in a group of leaders, could be valuable. The incongruency between leadership norms and traditional feminine stereotypes continues—there is no evidence that suggests that people believe women have the necessary traits to rule alone—and yet there seems to be a strong sentiment that women bring a voice of honesty and inclusion to governance.

THEORY OF THE INCONGRUITY BENEFIT: STRATEGIC FEMINIZATION BY ASSOCIATION

In addition to understanding how these stereotypes affect the political success of women themselves, one should also consider the impact of women's presence on the citizens' perception of the institution with which the women are associated. There is a general recognition in the literature on candidate selection that the traits of individual candidates influence the image of the party as a whole, which in turn triggers party elites to prioritize candidates with certain characteristics when making candidate selection decisions. As Hazan and Rahat (2010) explain, "a party's candidates will help *define its characteristics*—demographically, geographically, and ideologically—more than its organization or even its manifesto" (p. 6, emphasis mine). This means, therefore, that candidate traits are utilized by voters as information shortcuts about the party itself, not only triggering assumptions about the behavior of the candidate but also about the goals, direction, and priorities of the party as a whole.

Existing literature demonstrates the effects of women's presence on the citizens' perception of the institution, with a particular focus on the effect of women's descriptive representation on the perceived level of corruption. For example, Schwindt-Bayer (2010) finds a significant relationship between the citizens' perception of corruption and the presence of gender quotas. Using the 2006 Americas Barometer, she offers evidence that those citizens who live in a country with gender quotas perceive less corruption in government compared with those in countries without quotas.[10] Further, Barnes and Beaulieu (2014) offer evidence for a causal link between the perception of corruption and women's presence through their use of an experimental survey design. They find that the presence of a women candidate in an electoral contest decreases the suspicion of fraud in the election by 8–10% (p. 373). Esarey and Schwindt-Bayer (2017) also find evidence that the higher presence of women in the legislature is associated with a lower perception of corruption, though they note that this relationship is dependent on the level of electoral accountability in the state.

Beyond the effect of women's presence on the citizens' perception of corruption in the institution, there is also evidence that women's presence changes the citizens' level of trust in the institution. Using an experimental design in which they vary the gender balance on a hypothetical legislative committee, Clayton et al. (2018) find that women's presence on the committee is positively correlated with respondent assessments of fairness and trust in both the committee and decision-making process in general. In addition, Schwindt-Bayer and Alles (2018) use LAPOP survey questions on democratic support and performance to demonstrate that the presence of women in the legislature—just their presence alone—causes citizens to express "more support for democracy, greater satisfaction with democracy, more trust in the legislature, and they perceive a clear government (less corruption) when more women are in the national legislature" (p. 70). It seems, therefore, that the presence of women changes how people view the institution in which they serve; the institution is, in part, gendered by its inhabitants.

Because of the relationship between women's presence and the assumed traits of the institution, I argue that rational opportunists see a benefit to women's presence that has yet to be recognized in the literature. That is, because the inclusion of women triggers citizens to assume that an institution is more honest and democratic, women's presence can be used to strategically signal these traits. Under normal conditions, this association may be costly to the party or government due to the incongruity cost; in other words, citizens are not looking for feminized parties under normal circumstances. However, when the political context changes and temporarily inflates the value of these feminized traits, feminization of the party or government can be an asset, thereby changing the rational opportunist's inclusion calculation.

Specifically, I argue that strategic feminization is most likely to occur under conditions of declining legitimacy and thus that women's presence can be used to cultivate legitimacy under certain conditions. Legitimacy, as Weber (1968) explained, refers to the perception by citizens that those in power deserve their power. When a government is perceived as legitimate, citizens are more likely to comply with political authorities and laws without the threat of force; citizens, in short, are more likely to voluntarily obey the directives of the state when they view the government as legitimate. And, while it's possible to scare the citizens into obeying—that is, to rule with coercion—it is much easier and more sustainable for a government to foster at least some legitimacy in the eyes of its citizens (Tyler 2006).

There are several ways that governments can cultivate a perception of legitimacy, but one of the most prominent is to demonstrate that the government is "trustworthy" (Levi et al. 2009). A regime can signal its trustworthiness by submitting to constraints on its behavior; a democracy, for example, signals that there are constraints on the behavior of the governing elites because, if they ignore the will of the people, it allows the possibility that the elites could be punished in the next election. In addition, Levi et al. (2009) note that "some leaders are able to persuade citizens they are trustworthy by force of character, charisma, or reference to their *personal traits*, histories, and identities" (p. 357, my emphasis). In other words, a government can cultivate legitimacy by linking themselves to leaders whose personal traits are associated with trustworthiness. The connection to women here is clear: because of the assumed if/then relationship between women and democracy, as well as the powerful and consistent stereotype that women are more honest than men, women's presence in a political party or government will cultivate legitimacy.

It should not be assumed, however, that the potential benefit from the presence of women will drive governments and political parties to associate themselves with scores of women. There are two powerful disincentives to this strategy. First, as discussed in chapter 2, there are many costs associated with women's inclusion, arguably the most powerful being that it is rational for political actors to prevent competition. Thus, by limiting the power and access of women, women's presence in office is never completely normalized. This, in turn, constrains the ability of women to compete, thereby maintaining the patriarchal power structure. Second, as discussed earlier in this chapter, women are associated with many traits and behaviors that are not considered ideal for leadership. And, when they do demonstrate a leadership trait traditionally viewed as masculine—such as confidence—the backlash is immediate and substantial. Thus, a political party or government that places substantial numbers of women in power may encounter the public perception that they have become too weak or maternal to rule effectively or, if the women are demonstrating traditionally masculine traits, citizens may feel uncomfortable because of the violation of gender role expectations. It is more accurate to therefore characterize the potential role of the incongruity benefit as impacting, but not determining, the calculation of inclusion.

An obvious question at this point is "why women?" Part of the answer to this is simple: no other group is so consistently stereotyped as honest and supportive of democracy. But one could argue that, if a government is looking to signal, for example, inclusion and cooperation, another way of doing so would be to reserve seats in the legislature for an under-represented ethnic group. Yet this alternative strategy has the potential to be costly because political parties based on ethnic identities tend to prioritize increasing the power or sovereignty of their ethnic group (Htun 2004). Thus, their inclusion means that the government may need to compromise and make a policy change that decreases its own power; the symbolism of inclusion and cooperation, in this scenario, is likely to lead to actual inclusion and cooperation. Women are therefore the more palatable "other" because of their potential similarity to men. Ironically, even though women are perceived as being fundamentally similar to one another, they are actually so diverse that a political party or government can easily find women who sincerely support the goals of that party or government, even if it is fundamentally corrupt, authoritarian, and/or misogynistic. In other words, as Htun (2004) noted in her analysis of gender quotas and reserved seats, "unlike ethnic groups, women transcend geographic, occupational, language, and religious categories. In France, this meant that, in theory, women's representation would not threaten the republican universalist tradition" (p. 448). Women's presence, in short, does not actually pose a threat to the status quo, even though their presence may be interpreted as just that.

CONCLUSION

While women's roles have changed in recent decades, the stereotypes that women are more honest, cooperative, and just naturally democratic appear to be holding strong. And yet, because women's involvement in the political sphere has become less objectionable over time, these traits carry a new political value. It is no longer completely unacceptable to be a woman in government, and it is actually an asset, I argue, when the government or political party is losing legitimacy due to perceived dishonesty or lack of commitment to democratic ideals. This does not mean that women are perceived as equal to men—all countries continue to be patriarchies and women's communal traits are typically viewed as incongruent with leadership—but it does mean that sometimes the assumed incongruous traits of women can be a temporary boon to themselves as well as their political parties.

In the next chapter, I offer the first set of my empirical analyses. Using a mix of case studies and regression analyses results as evidence, I argue that the increased number of women candidates in most post-corruption-scandal environments is due to temporary changes in the elites' inclusion calculation. These changes, in turn, potentially make women's increased presence advantageous to existing male elites, but not always—the other variables in the inclusion calculation determine whether the incongruity benefit is "enough" to merit women's inclusion. Specifically, I offer case studies of post-corruption elections in Ireland, Portugal, and Spain, and explain that, while the incongruity benefit was high in all three contexts, it was not high enough to trigger women's inclusion in all three countries.

In addition, I present regression analyses that examine the correlation between an election fought in the context of revelations of substantial government scandals and the number of women who win legislative seats, and I find evidence that citizens are more likely to vote for women in the post-scandal environment. Elites, therefore, have an incentive to "strategically feminize" in order to associate their parties with women's assumed traits after a massive scandal breaks.

The Strategic Use
of Women Candidates
in Post-Scandal Environments

INTRODUCTION

When a massive political corruption scandal is revealed, the legitimacy of the government is shaken to its core. Take, for example, a scenario in which many sitting members of the government and/or legislature are accused of accepting bribes in exchange for favorable policy decisions. This accusation of bribery goes beyond everyday clientelism—this is not just greasing the wheels, but rather is a clear tit-for-tat exchange that implicates several high-ranking leaders of the state. In this scenario, citizens' worst fears about their government are confirmed; it becomes undeniable that their elected representatives broke a foundational principle of democracy by putting their own personal desires in front of the needs of their constituents. Even minor levels of corruption erode the legitimacy of the government (Seligson 2002), but this—this is the kind of scandal revelation that will damage the legitimacy of the government for years. And thus, this is the moment when, I argue, the strategic value of women increases dramatically; in this particular context, when a government is brought to its knees by a massive political scandal, feminization is a potential solution to the loss of legitimacy.

In this chapter, I examine from three angles the effect that the revelation of a corruption scandal has on women's inclusion. First, I present an analysis of the selection of women candidates in the post-scandal context, with a particular focus on Spain and Portugal. Next, I consider candidate selection in Ireland and discuss the reasons why the corruption scandal there—and the resulting incongruity benefit—was not enough to trigger increases in women's inclusion. Finally, I consider the voter response to women candidates in the post-scandal environment and offer a large-N regression analysis of legislative electoral results over a period of 20 years. Overall, my results suggest that, under most circumstances, the revelation of a massive corruption scandal creates a strong incentive for elites to associate their parties with women, thereby driving them to increase the presence of women candidates on the party lists.

AN EXAMINATION OF PARTY NOMINATION BEHAVIOR

In the vast majority of countries, party elites at either the local or national level have the power of deciding which aspiring candidates (or, aspirants) become the actual candidates who run under the party label. While we are aware of a number of factors that party elites seek out in prospective candidates, including previous electoral experience, local roots in a particular region or district, and/or familial relation to previously elected officials, we know relatively little about the conditions under which elites choose women as candidates. Here, I argue that a massive corruption scandal affects the likelihood that elites will select women as candidates, but this is not necessarily enough to guarantee their inclusion. Specifically, I propose that a severe corruption scandal changes an element of the incongruity cost into a benefit, thereby creating an incentive for rational opportunist party elites to potentially select more women for their candidate lists. Women's inclusion, I argue, becomes a valuable strategy in this environment due to their association with honesty and democracy; without actually changing any of the factors that led to the corruption scandal, elites see an opportunity to use women's inclusion as a means to repair the reputation of the party or government. However, this potential benefit is not always enough to trigger women's inclusion; the costs in the inclusion calculation can, under certain circumstances, be too high for elites to be comfortable with a strategy of increasing the presence of women on the lists.

Spain, Portugal, and Ireland provide excellent opportunities for a close analysis of the effect of scandal on the selection decisions of party elites, as well as the constraints of institutions on their selection strategies. In some ways, these countries are quite similar in having advanced industrial economies with a historically Roman Catholic citizenry. In addition, while politics in these countries include some patron-client behavior and incidents of corruption, all three are relatively well-functioning democracies in which massive governmental scandals or malfeasance are anomalies. However, their institutional structures vary significantly, offering an opportunity to see how the other variables in the inclusion calculation—threat and displacement costs, for example—can potentially outweigh the incongruity benefit in the post-scandal context. While political parties in Spain and Portugal have relatively centralized nomination procedures (Montabes and Ortega 1999; Lundell 2004), Ireland does not. Candidate selection in Ireland is "territorially decentralized—sometimes to even lower levels than those of the small multimember district" (Hazan and Rahat 2010, p. 138). Their respective electoral systems further reinforce this power dynamic: Spain and Portugal both employ closed-list PR systems with a relatively low incentive to cultivate a personal vote, while Ireland uses the Single Transferable Vote (STV) system. The STV system generates a strong incentive to cultivate a high personal vote and thus, just as one would predict, the incumbency advantage is incredibly strong in Ireland. Thus, the institutional conditions in Spain and Portugal create an incentive for party leaders to increase the presence of women candidates; the selectorate in these countries, in other words, sees an advantage to responding to a post-scandal environment with a unique and temporary strategy of increasing women's inclusion. In Ireland, however, the institutional conditions raise the threat and displacement costs so much that, even in the post-scandal electoral context, the inclusion calculation does not result in an overall benefit to strategically feminizing the party.

Each country's relationship with international organizations also varied during this time. Arguably, the EU is the most relevant IO for these three countries during this period of their history, so my analyses of the potential international responsiveness benefit center on that relationship. Their respective relationships with the EU differ from one another: Ireland could be viewed as the least interested in signaling commitment to the norms of this organization, while Portugal and Spain had more incentives to demonstrate their adherence to the goals of European integration. The possible impact of the international realm on women's inclusion is therefore different across these three cases.

In the next section, I examine the party nomination behavior of the major parties in Spain, Portugal, and Ireland. I begin each country analysis with a description of the corruption scandals revealed before the election year in question and then consider the theoretical values of the inclusion calculation variables in each country context. Next, I present the percentage of women candidates nominated by each party in the election year closest to the scandal, as well as the election before and after it (if available).[1] In addition, for the closed-list systems of Spain and Portugal, I present the percentage of lists with women at the head of the list—the number one list position—a position which offers a particularly high likelihood of winning as well as a high level of visibility. The results suggest that, while a corruption scandal is enough to propel party elites to increase women's inclusion in Spain and Portugal, the unique institutional structure of Ireland creates high threat and displacement costs which, in the eyes of elites, outweigh the benefits of women's inclusion.

SPAIN

While the people of Spain have experienced incidents of government corruption in the past (particularly under the Franco regime), the number and severity of the corruption scandals before the 1996 election were unprecedented. The first publicized corruption concerned Mariano Rubio, a former governor of the Bank of Spain who played a significant role in developing Spain's economic policies and who was accused of tax fraud in 1994. This was not the first accusation of fraud against Rubio—only a few months before, he had been accused of providing confidential economic information to a small investment bank that shortly thereafter collapsed. Soon after the charges against Rubio were filed, he was arrested and sent to prison. In response, Carlos Solchaga, minister of the economy, resigned his seat in parliament due to his close relationship to and well-known support of Rubio.

Also in 1994, Luis Roldán, head of the Civil Guard, was arrested for bribery and misappropriation of funds in a scandal unrelated to the Rubio affair. Within weeks of his arrest, Roldán escaped from custody and fled the country (he was later caught and arrested again but was out of the country for several weeks). The PSOE (Partido Socialista Obrero Español) government was accused of allowing Roldán to escape because he threatened to expose the corruption of other members, and thus Antonio Asunción, the minister of the interior, resigned in response. Roldán did indeed expose more corruption, accusing, after his arrest, José Luis Corcuera, the minster of justice, of playing a key part in his system of illegal funding and bribery, causing Corcuera to resign. In response to all of the publicized political corruption in 1994, Baltasar Garzon resigned as head of the national anti-drug campaign and from his seat in the Congreso. Garzon was a former judge with a reputation for honesty and resigned from the government due to what he referred to as Prime Minister Gonzalez's "passive attitude" to corruption.[2]

The year 1995 brought with it the most explosive corruption scandal yet: the GAL scandal, also known as the Dirty War. Early in the year, an investigation began into accusations that, in the mid-1980s, the PSOE government was directly involved in the murders of 23 members of the Basque separatist group ETA. The accusations charged the ministry of the interior with using a secret fund to create and fund the GAL (Grupos Antiterroristas de Liberación), an anti-terrorist liberation group implicated in death-squad killings. Jose Barrionuevo and José Luis Corcuera, former ministers under Prime Minister Gonzalez during this period, were accused of being involved in the GAL kidnappings and the payment of hush money. Witnesses within the government testified that the death-squad killings were officially organized and condoned, and Rafael Vera, the former state secretary of security, was jailed for covering up GAL activity.

During that same year, 1995, Deputy Prime Minister Narcs Serra, Minister of Defense Julian Garca Vargas, and the chief of Spain's secret service, Emilio Alonso Manglano, also resigned after it was revealed that many government figures, including King Juan Carlos, had their phones illegally tapped by the Spanish intelligence service. In addition, the Filesa affair concluded in 1995 with 39 people charged with illegal financing, including a former PSOE treasurer and several bank chairmen. One month before the 1996 legislative election, Prime Minister Gonzalez was interviewed for the newspaper *El Mundo* and acknowledged the damage that had been done, saying "if it were not for corruption, we would win the election relatively easily."[3] As expected, his party, the PSOE, did not win a plurality of the vote, and the Partido Popular (PP) in coalition with the moderate Catalan Nationalists (CiU) took over the government.

Spain: Variables in the Inclusion Calculation

In the months leading up to the 1996 legislative election, the variables in the inclusion calculations of party elites likely yielded an overall benefit for increasing women's inclusion. Specifically, I argue that, in addition to the impact of the incongruity benefit, the displacement, threat, and incongruity costs were low, and the domestic responsiveness benefits for the PSOE were substantial. Also, in accordance with the consensus in the existing literature on Spain, it is likely that the women in proximity played an important role in this increase and, because the PSOE was a member of both an international socialist organization and the EU, there was also an international responsiveness benefit. Thus, I expect the presence of women on the party lists, as well as the number of women at the top of those lists, to be higher in the first post-scandal election.

In this environment of unprecedented revelations of corruption, the incongruity benefit associated with increasing the presence of women is substantial. That is, the benefits of associating the party with women's communal traits in this electoral context seem clear, particularly for the PSOE, the party most involved in the corruption scandals. Further, there is reason to believe that the citizens of Spain are especially likely to respond well to an increased presence of women under these conditions due to the association of women with "transformational leadership" in this country. Garcia-Retamero and López-Zafra (2006) offer a focused analysis of stereotypes in Spain and find evidence that, while there continues to be prejudice against women who work in industries incongruent with their gender roles (i.e., an incongruity cost), there is also evidence that people assume women's leadership style to be "transformational." In contrast to the "transactional" method which rests on status quo and tangible rewards, the transformational style "involves establishing oneself as a role model by gaining the *trust* and confidence of followers" (p. 52, my emphasis) as well as rethinking conventional practices. Thus, due to the frequency and severity of the corruption scandal revelations in this environment, it is reasonable for a rational opportunist to see the value in increasing the presence of women in order to trigger the citizens of Spain to believe that corrupt practices will be replaced by a more honest, careful, and thoughtful style of representation. However, while I argue that the incongruity benefit was substantial in this post-scandal context, this variable alone is not strong enough to trigger an increase in the inclusion of women in the legislature. Instead, the other costs and benefits are also important to determining if the incongruity benefit will be substantial *enough* to merit women's increased presence.

The incongruity cost of running women candidates during this period was considerable, but not as powerful as one might assume from Spain's history and cultural heritage. That being said, it is only recently that things have not been rather grim for women in Spain. The Spanish civil war isolated Spain from the rest of Europe, thereby preventing the cultural modernization of gender roles that began elsewhere on the continent in the early twentieth century. Further, Franco's regime exacerbated the power of traditional gender-role expectations by requiring that women get permission from their father or husband to work outside the home or even make an important life decision (Lopez-Zafra and Garcia-Retamero 2012). In addition, Spain is a traditionally Catholic country, and thus popular ideas about gender roles were initially slow to change. However, since the end of Franco's rule, women's status in Spain has changed substantially and, particularly in the eyes of young people, there is now more flexibility in women's stereotyped traits. The stereotypes of women's roles and traits in Spain, in other words, have shifted dramatically over the past few decades, such that now, people are more likely than ever before to associate women with some agentic traits (López-Sáez et al. 2008; Lopez-Zafra and Garcia-Retamero 2012). In this cultural context, therefore, the incongruity cost should be conceived as present but not overwhelming.

Two of the other potentially daunting costs in the inclusion calculation—the displacement and threat costs—were also low during this time. Both the design of the electoral system for the legislative lower house and the PSOE's candidate selection method had negative effects on the displacement cost: the Congreso de los Diputados employed a closed-list electoral system, and the PSOE utilized a centralized method of candidate selection throughout the 1990s (Lundell 2004; Montabes and Ortega 1999). This electoral system creates a low incentive to cultivate a personal vote, which means the cost of replacing male incumbents with women is relatively low. Further, the district magnitudes across the country are generally high—for example, the district including Madrid has a magnitude of 34 seats—which also decreases the displacement cost of adding women to the lists. In addition, candidate selection decisions were made at the national level of the party elite, not at the local or regional level, though the regional level could make suggestions or requests. The final factor driving down the displacement cost was the context of unprecedented corruption revelations. In this environment, incumbency loses value (Klašnja 2015), and thus the cost of removing male incumbents and replacing them with women drops dramatically. Further, the threat cost of women's increased inclusion should also be seen as relatively low in this context. The centralized leadership and selection mechanism of the

PSOE means that the elites of this party are insulated; it is challenging to move up through the ranks quickly in this system and also difficult for legislators to exert substantial influence on the party elite. Thus, the addition of women to the candidate lists does not trigger a direct threat to their leadership, thereby suggesting a low threat cost.

As discussed in chapter 2, the primary determinant of whether domestic responsiveness will trigger a cost or a benefit in the inclusion calculus is the ideological position of the party. The PSOE—the party implicated in most of the corruption scandals—is a center-left party that most easily fits into the social democrat party family (Clucas and Valdini 2015, p. 96). Similar to other European parties in this family, the PSOE originally had strong roots in Marxism and protecting workers, but shifted more toward the ideological center in the late twentieth century. This means that the PSOE of today is generally to the left of center on social issues (e.g., they have been vocal supporters of gay marriage and of more generally limiting the influence of the Catholic church on social policy) and more in the center on economic issues; in short, they are a mainstream party of the center-left. Because of this ideology, their voters are unlikely to be alienated or upset by the increased presence of women candidates in the party. On the contrary, PSOE elites should anticipate a domestic responsiveness benefit; an increase in women's inclusion should be well received due to this party's ideological stances on modernization and equality.

In addition, a potential international responsiveness benefit was also available to the PSOE because of their membership in the IO Socialist International (SI) as well as Spain's membership in the EU. As just described, the PSOE should not be considered "socialist" in terms of the traditional Marxian understanding as it has moved into the mainstream, center-left position in its party system. That being said, the PSOE continues to be an important and influential member of the SI. Thus, in 1994, when the executive council of the SI asked all of its member parties to increase their women candidates by a minimum of 10% in every election (Threlfall 2007, p. 1082), it seems likely that this influenced the PSOE elites when composing their candidate lists. Further, the PSOE is generally a strong supporter of European integration, so much so that critics have alleged that it prioritizes and legitimizes its domestic priorities by framing them as necessary to meet the demands of the EU (Holman 1996; Closa and Heywood 2004). Thus, following the EU policy directives on gender equality by increasing the presence of women in the party is a simple way of demonstrating its continuing commitment to the EU. That being said, one should not expect the international responsiveness benefit in this context to be substantial—that is, there is no clear cost to ignoring the requests of the SI or the EU gender policy directives and no clear benefit to following them, so this element was probably a small influence in the rational opportunist calculation.

Finally, while not a variable in the inclusion calculation, the women in proximity—both in and around the leadership of the PSOE—are an important factor in tipping the balance in favor of women's inclusion. As Threlfall (2007) explains, the presence of party feminists inside the PSOE is crucial to understanding any outcome in this party that increases the presence of women. The feminist caucus within this party—Mujer y Socialismo—had been active in proposing party gender quotas since 1979 and, while they were not a part of the leadership making selection decisions, it would be false to portray the feminist wing of the party as weak. Instead, they were a steady drumbeat for women's increased inclusion on the lists and in leadership for years and seemed able to make headway in the context of the 1996 election.

That being said, it is important to also reflect upon the many years that the Mujer y Socialismo was not able to make headway on their goal of increased inclusion of women. That is, women's presence in the party, even when there are a few women at the upper echelons of party leadership, does not guarantee an increase in women's inclusion on candidate lists. In her analysis of intra-party politics in Spain, Threlfall (2007) specifically engages this issue and explains:

> While the presence of women party activists can be effective in generating movement towards the adoption of the gender representation rule, even women members of executive committees cannot force through implementation of a conference decision. They may

well have no direct say in candidate selection, being usually con-
fined to a specific party unit such as the Secretariat for Membership/
Organisation or an ad hoc electoral committee. (P. 1072)

This is a critical point to emphasize because, as I discuss at length in the
concluding chapter, women's presence does not equal women's power.
Thus, just because there are women in the party or even women in leadership in the party, we cannot assume that they will necessarily have the
power to exert influence over candidate selection decisions. At the end of
the day, the level of women's inclusion in the candidate lists in Spain rested
on the ultimate decision of male party elites.

To examine the effect of massive corruption on the selection decisions
of party elites, I collected the candidate lists of the major parties from
every district for three legislative elections in Spain: 1993, 1996, and 2000.[4]
Each data point, therefore, is the percentage of women on each party list
in each district. It is important to note that there were no legislated gender
quotas that required, for example, a certain percentage of women on the
lists during the years of this analysis. There were voluntary party quotas
employed throughout this time period by the PSOE and IU (Izquierda
Unida), but these quotas were relatively low and not very powerful—25%
of candidates and no placement mandates—and also remained stable in
the 1993 and 1996 elections.[5]

Table 4.1 offers evidence that the corruption scandals leading up
to the 1996 legislative election did indeed impact the candidate selection decisions. Compared to the lists of 1993, the percentage of women
candidates increased substantially in all parties, with a particularly high
increase in the PSOE—the party involved in the vast majority of corruption scandals. Of particular importance is the increase in the number of
party lists with women in the first position on the list. This is a highly
coveted, very public list position; the top of the list is the position most
likely to lead to election *and* the most visible to voters. Further, the top list
position is also considered a signaling device to voters; the person in that
top spot "represents the image the party wants to give of itself" (Espírito-
Santo and Sanches 2018, p. 117). This is also a notoriously difficult position
for women candidates to secure. In her discussion of candidate selection

Table 4.1 WOMEN'S PRESENCE AND POSITION IN CANDIDATE LISTS IN SPAIN

Election Year	Party	Average Percentage of Women on Lists* (%)	Percent of Lists with Woman in First Position on Party List (%)
1993	IU	32.3	10.0
	PP	18.6	7.8
	PSOE	31.2	8.0
1996	**IU**	**40.2**	**14.0**
	PP	**22.6**	**11.7**
	PSOE	**40.0**	**16.0**
2000	IU	42.9	11.0
	PP	31.6	15.6
	PSOE	47.2	19.6

* Averages include party coalitions, such as IU-CA or IU-EB.

NOTE: Election Results in bold occurred in the post-corruption scandal environment.

SOURCE OF CANDIDATE LISTS: Agencia Estatal Boletín Oficial del Estado (https://www.boe.es/) and Junta Electoral Central (http://www.juntaelectoralcentral.es/).

and election of women in Spain, Threlfall (2005) notes that "A woman heading a slate is a good indicator, and probably the strongest available, of women's political power in a party, though it is also the *most infrequently found*" (136, emphasis mine). If a party, therefore, wants to "feminize" its image after a corruption scandal, then placing more women in the most prominent position is a likely strategic response.

Because there is a 100% increase in the number of PSOE lists with women in the first position between 1993 and 1996, this evidence suggests that the selectorate strategically placed women at the top and most visible position in order to associate women with the party. Further, while the candidate lists for the following election (2000) continue to demonstrate an upward trajectory, the rate of increase dramatically slowed and one party, the IU, actually decreased the number of women in the first position on the list. Thus, because the PSOE increased the inclusion of women so dramatically in the post-corruption election, this suggests that the calculation of inclusion was influenced by the high incongruity benefit in this electoral context.

PORTUGAL

It is shocking for citizens to watch any former member of government be arrested, but it is particularly disconcerting when the person arrested was recently prime minister. So when, in 2014, former Prime Minister Jose Socrates was arrested at Lisbon airport on suspicion of tax fraud, money laundering, and corruption, it was deeply disturbing for the people of Portugal.[6] The various accusations of financial malfeasance against Socrates span a time frame of over 10 years, and include using a bank account in his mother's name to launder money. The situation was not resolved quickly; Socrates remained in police custody until September 2015 when he was transferred out of prison and into house arrest, and he remains under investigation to this day.

In the same month that Socrates was arrested, another substantial corruption scandal broke: the "Golden Visa" scandal. While it is an accepted government policy of Portugal (and many other countries) to offer residence permits in exchange for in-country investments of at least €500,000, the police arrested 11 people on November 13, 2014, including the head of Portugal's border agency, on suspicion of receiving personal pay-offs to provide permits. Three days later, the interior minister, Miguel Macedo, resigned from office in response. In addition, the deputy prime minister, Paulo Portas, was brought in for questioning by a parliamentary committee, but was never charged.[7]

Both of the major parties in Portugal were impacted by these scandals: Socrates was a prime minister of the Partido Socialista (PS) government of 2004–2011, and those accused in the Golden Visa scandal were from the coalition of the Partido Social Democrata (PPD/PSD) and Partido Popular (CDS-PP) government elected in 2011. Unlike in the Spanish election discussed earlier, however, the corruption issues did not take center stage. Instead, economic and migration issues seemed to be the focal points of the campaigns (Goulart and Veiga 2016). This is not to say that the corruption did not matter to voters, but rather that Portugal, unlike Spain, represents a case with a more gentle break in the status quo. Elites in both parties could still have had an incentive to select more women to run as candidates in the legislative election of 2015—after all, these were major allegations that tarnished the reputations of both major parties, and both occurred within a year of the upcoming election. And yet it is also possible that the corruption was not powerful enough to trigger a substantial increase in the incongruity benefit, and thus the inclusion calculation may not favor the inclusion of more women. In the following section, I consider the theoretical values of the variables in the inclusion calculation in this context and discuss the likely costs and benefits to existing elites of increasing the presence of women.

Portugal: Variables in the Inclusion Calculation

As in Spain, the incongruity cost of including women in politics in Portugal has changed dramatically over the twentieth century, during most of which the state enacted and enforced legal restrictions that actively prevented women's equality. For example, in 1967, a new civil code was adopted that required authorization from a husband or father before a woman could apply for a job, leave the country, or even move out of the home (Ferreira 2011). However, after the authoritarian regime came to an end in 1974, the culture surrounding women's roles shifted. The restrictions on women's lives propagated by the previous regime became symbols of its authoritarian and hyper-traditional style, and thus the cultural rejection of authoritarianism carried with it a rejection of the traditional gender roles previously enforced by the state. As Ferreira (2011) explains in her analysis of this time period in Portugal:

> Legal changes were made without opposition. For this reason women did not have to mobilize . . . The political elite acted as though the principle of equality was nothing more than a natural part of the process of democratic modernization. (P. 171)

Thus, the association of traditional roles with the previous regime triggered an inadvertent change in norms surrounding gender roles. This, in turn, caused a shift in how citizens viewed women leaders, thereby lowering the incongruity cost. This is not to say that there was no longer a potential cost to women's inclusion; Baum and Espírito-Santo (2012) present survey results from the public-opinion data of Freire and Viegas (2009) and demonstrate that 44.5% of men agreed with the statement that "men make better political leaders than women do." But it does suggest that the culture surrounding gender roles has shifted in recent years, and thus that the incongruity cost of including women, particularly in left-wing parties, was not overwhelming.

In addition, the association of women with a well-functioning democracy seems to have held across the decades, thereby suggesting a potential incongruity benefit, under the right circumstances. Again using the Freire and Viegas (2009) data, Baum and Espírito-Santo (2012) offer evidence that the Portuguese electorate continues to associate women and democracy, even more than 40 years after their democratic transition. They note that 55.8% of women and 36.5% of men agreed with the statement that "the fact that 80% of MPs are men is a serious threat to democracy" (p. 332) and, while that is not a majority of all citizens surveyed, the wording of the question is so extreme that these results are remarkable. That is, this was not a tentative question that asked about representational preferences or whether this balance was a problem, but rather whether the gender balance of the legislature was a "serious threat to democracy." And even with that extreme wording, more than half of the women respondents agreed. This signals that women's presence is still associated with democracy, and thus that there is a potential incongruity benefit here.

As described in chapter 2, one of the most powerful determinants of the threat cost is the level of decentralization in candidate selection. Because the candidate selection process of political parties is highly centralized in Portugal (Van Biezen 2003; Lisi 2015), the threat cost of increased inclusion of female legislative candidates is low. Some parties do include a requirement to consult with the local-level leadership in their official party statutes, but the norm of a low adherence to official party rules as well as the vagueness of these internal rules causes a substantial difference between the process as outlined and the actual candidate selection practice of party leadership. As Lisi (2015) explains, this divergence between rules and practice has a powerful consequence for candidate selection because it "strengthens [the power] of the leadership and especially the party inner core which coalesces around the leader" (p. 47); the centralized core of national-level party leaders, in other words, should be considered the first and last word on candidate selection in Portugal. Further, even when the local level is granted the power to request and negotiate certain candidates for the lists, the national-level leadership sends them explicit criteria for the selection of possible candidates according to their "strategic considerations" regarding the ideal balance of age, gender, occupation, and other personal traits of the prospective candidates (Lisi 2015, p. 103). Therefore, because of the highly centralized nature of this process, the threat cost of increased inclusion is low; the increased presence of women legislators does not pose a threat to the power of the centralized and exclusive leadership making the decisions.

On first blush, one might characterize the displacement cost in the Portuguese electoral context as low. The electoral system used by their unicameral parliament, the Assembleia da República, is a closed list PR, and this triggers a low incentive to cultivate a personal vote due to the lack of opportunity for voters to vote directly for a particular candidate. Instead, voters cast a vote for the pre-ordered party lists, thereby making it relatively low cost for party elites to switch out candidates and even incumbents if they calculate the increased presence of women as valuable. However, Shugart et al. (2005) note that the district magnitude has an important effect on the incentive to cultivate a personal vote, even in a closed list PR system. And, as Espírito-Santo and Sanches (2018) explain in their analysis of the personal vote in Portugal, while the average district magnitude is relatively high at 11 seats per district, the variation is substantial—some districts have as few as 2 seats and another, Lisbon, currently elects 47 seats (p. 119). Thus, because there is substantial variation in district magnitude in Portugal, one should anticipate some intra-country variation in the displacement cost as well. This cost variation will not be extreme—it is indeed safe to characterize Portugal as carrying a relatively low displacement cost in the calculation of inclusion—but it is important to recognize that this cost is not uniform across the country.[8]

The domestic responsiveness benefit for increasing the presence of women in the party was not substantial but, particularly for the Partido Socialista (PS)—the main center-left party in the system—the inclusion of more women would not be met with dismay from voters. That being said, women's organizations in this country were "fragile" and the rise of a national women's movement in Portugal had been limited (Monteiro and Ferreira 2016, p. 474). Thus, it is unlikely that elites saw women's inclusion as necessary to address domestic concerns about women's power. After all, the big advances in women's rights during the transition to democracy had more to do with the symbolic meaning of equality in the new democracy rather than a government response to citizen demands for women's rights (Ferreira 2011).

The influence of the international realm—and specifically the EU— was also a consideration, though the potential international responsiveness benefit was not clear. On the one hand, Portuguese governments in the past had strategically adopted policies that reflected the EU norms on gender equality so as to demonstrate that they were "good students" and therefore deserving of economic aid (Melo 2017, p. 270). Further, there is evidence that the adoption of a gender quota in 2006 was, in part, due to the influence of international recommendations (Baum and Espírito-Santo 2012). Thus, increasing the presence of women on the lists could once again serve as a signal of support of EU integration goals. However, there is also evidence that Portuguese elites tended to resist international pressure to reform gender equity policies, as shown by the time lags between various gender equity proposals suggested by the EU and the resulting domestic policy (Monteiro and Ferreira 2016). Thus, it seems best to assume that this potential benefit effect was present but not powerful.

Regarding the role of women in proximity, there is limited evidence that the women leaders in even the center-left PS had direct influence over candidate selection decisions. As Verge and Espírito-Santo (2016) note in their discussion of the Partido Socialista:

although the leader of the women's section (of the PS) also sits on the main party bodies at all party levels and has been charged with supervising the implementation of the party quota in 1998 . . . she does not participate in the crucial informal arrangements between the presidents of the district-level branches and the central party leader who initially draft the lists . . . So the women's section has no influence in candidate selection. (P. 432)

This is not to say that the women in proximity had no effect—there could be indirect influence—but rather that if they did engineer the increase in women candidates in 2015, their methods for doing so are unclear.

To examine the effect of these scandals on the selection of women as candidates, I collected the candidate lists from Portugal in 2011 and 2015. Again, I limited the data set to the two major parties in the country, and each data point is the percentage of women on the party list of each district. Unlike Spain, Portugal has a legislative gender quota requiring political parties to select a certain number of women candidates. However, this quota law was adopted in 2006 and no changes were made in the years leading up to the 2011 or 2015 elections that could have impacted those results. In both of these elections, candidate lists were required to include 33% from both genders and also to "zipper" the candidates such that there are no two candidates of the same gender in consecutive order. Further, the penalties for non-compliance also remained the same (Baum and Espírito-Santo 2012). Thus, while a gender quota impacted the nomination behaviors of party elites in both of these elections, there is no reason to believe that the quota exerted a different effect in one year versus the other.

The evidence presented in table 4.2 suggests that party elites responded to the post-scandal environment by altering their nomination strategies for women candidates. All parties increased the percentage of women candidates on their lists, though the pre-election right-wing coalition of the PPD/PSD and CDS-PP increased their women candidates more than the PS. Perhaps more telling, all parties dramatically increased the number of women running at the top of their lists. PS doubled the number

Table 4.2 WOMEN'S PRESENCE AND POSITION IN CANDIDATE LISTS IN PORTUGAL

Election Year	Party	Average Percentage of Women on Lists	Percent of Lists with Woman in First Position on Party List
2011	PS	35.8	13.0
	PPD/PSD	28.3	8.7
	CDS-PP	32.0	22.7
2015	**PS**	**37.5**	**26.1**
	PPD/PSD. CDS-PP	**39.6**	**30.4**

NOTE: Election Results in bold occurred in the post-corruption scandal environment.

SOURCE OF CANDIDATE LISTS: https://www.eleicoes.mai.gov.pt/legislativas2011/candidatos.html; https://www.eleicoes.mai.gov.pt/legislativas2015/candidatos.html.

of women in the first list position, jumping from 13% of lists with women at the top in 2011 to 26.1% of lists with women in the first position in 2015. And even more striking, a right-wing party in coalition—PPD/PSD— more than tripled the number of women holding the top list position. In 2011, 8.7% of their candidate lists were headed by women, but in 2015, 30.4% of their candidate lists placed women at the top of the list. Part of this increase is due to their coalition partner—CDS-PP—who offered 22.7% of lists with women at the head of the list in the previous election, but also suggests a conscious and strategic effort to make women the face of the party.

IRELAND

At no point in time has Ireland been without corruption scandals. From the Locke Distillery Scandal of 1947 to the tumultuous career of former Prime Minister Haughey, examples of political corruption are peppered throughout Irish history. That being said, the number of publicized political corruption scandals leading up to the 2002 legislative election is far and away the most extreme. Corruption of this severity and frequency had never before been witnessed, and most of the incidents involved the parties in the then-governing coalition: Fianna Fáil and the Progressive Democrats.

In the years before the 2002 election, so many scandals broke that the government had to create multiple tribunals to investigate all of the accusations. In May 1998, the Moriarty Tribunal investigated Hugh Coveney, former defense minister, for unreported monetary gifts. One week later, Coveney fell off of a cliff (it was never established whether the fall was suicide, murder, or accidental). Shortly after the creation of the Moriarty Tribunal, the Flood Tribunal was established to investigate Foreign Minister Ray Burke, who was accused of accepting a large, undeclared payment from a developer in exchange for granting planning permission for the development of 700 acres of land in Dublin. In addition, Burke was accused of selling Irish passports to a Saudi businessman while serving as minister of justice in 1990. Within weeks of the creation of this tribunal, Burke resigned. Through the testimony of developers, it was also revealed that 15 Dublin councilors had also accepted cash from a developer. The testimony indicated on record that these were bribes and that the councilors supported the new development in question only after receiving the money.[9]

The Flood Tribunal subsequently turned its attention to Padraig Flynn, the sole European Commissioner representing Ireland in the EU. Allegedly, Flynn received, failed to report, and kept a donation of IR£50,000 intended for his party, Fianna Fáil, in the 1980s. He denied this accusation, but the situation exploded when then-Prime Minister Bertie Ahern was accused of having knowledge of and neglecting to report Flynn's actions. Neither person ever admitted guilt, but the Flood Tribunal continued its investigation for several years. In May 2000, the Flood Tribunal determined that over a 17-year period in politics, former Prime Minister Haughey received gifts of more than IR£8 million.[10]

As the tribunals continued, several other political figures were accused and indicted on corruption charges. Denis Foley, a Fianna Fáil Teachta Dála (TD), resigned in 2000 after proof surfaced that he held offshore accounts containing undocumented, untaxed money. During this same period, another Fianna Fáil TD, Liam Lawlor, who was serving on the parliamentary ethics committee, was also accused of financial corruption and was sent to prison for refusing to cooperate with the Flood Tribunal's inquiries into the allegation. Shortly thereafter, Ned O'Keeffe, the minister of state with responsibility for food, resigned after it was revealed that he had failed to declare his ownership of a pig farm and feed mill. Not only had he voted on legislation that would affect his farm (without revealing his personal interest), but he also neglected to follow a "voluntary quality assurance scheme" created by the government to prevent the spread of disease between farms. Bobby Molloy, another minister of state and a member of the Progressive Democrats (the party in coalition with Fianna Fáil), was also forced to resign during this period due to accusations that he influenced the decisions of several high-ranking judges.[11]

IRELAND: VARIABLES IN THE INCLUSION CALCULATION

Because of the significant corruption scandals exposed in the lead up to the Irish legislative election of 2002, the potential incongruity benefit of including more women candidates was substantial. The leading party in the governing coalition, Fianna Fáil, could particularly benefit from the perception that they were reforming and embracing ideals of honesty; adding women candidates was a potentially simple way to signal change without having to reform any corrupt practices. However, while this potential benefit is high, it may not be high enough to merit women's increased presence. In the following section, I consider the other variables in the inclusion calculation and explain that, unlike in Spain and Portugal, the other variable values suggest that women's increased inclusion was too costly to the party elites and thus unlikely.

While the incongruity benefit is potentially high in this electoral context, the incongruity cost seems to be less of a factor. As McElroy and Marsh (2011) discuss in their analysis of Irish voter behavior, they find evidence that voters in this country are not unusually biased against women candidates. Instead, they offer evidence that female candidates in Ireland are "neither systematically favoured nor discriminated against by the voters" (p. 530). However, there is evidence that contradicts this finding and instead suggests that there is indeed bias against women candidates in this country. Schwindt-Bayer et al. (2010) explain:

> In Ireland, we found that voters discriminate against women, controlling for all else. When we interact gender with other determinants of electoral outcomes, we find that two of the individual characteristics that increase men's prospects do not give as big of a boost to women. Both being an incumbent and having previous electoral experience generate more votes for a candidate, but the increase is not as great for female candidates as it is for men. (P. 703)

The incongruity cost in Ireland, therefore, seems best conceptualized as being present but not unusually high. As in Portugal and Spain, there continue to be Irish voters with traditional views of women's roles and they, at times, react negatively to women's presence in the party. But this effect does not seem to be the most powerful variable in the inclusion calculation.

The displacement cost, on the other hand, is incredibly high in the Irish electoral context. Due to their legislative electoral system, removing male incumbents and replacing them with women is very costly to the party elites. Their unicameral legislature, Dáil Éireann, employs a single transferable vote system to elect its members. Because this electoral system asks voters to rank order the candidates on the ballot and the district magnitude is 3–5 seats per district, each party runs multiple candidates in every district. This means that the voter is faced with both inter- and intra-party competition, as well as the expectation that they will not only express their preferred candidates but actually rank these preferences. This is, in short, a candidate-centered system with a substantial incentive to cultivate a personal vote, and thus, in this context, the individual traits of the candidates are important to voters. Being an incumbent is therefore a significant advantage here (Shugart 1994) and in turn, party leaders face a steep cost for removing incumbents from the candidate lists and replacing them with women under any circumstances (Schwindt-Bayer 2005; McElroy and Marsh 2011; McGing 2013).

Further, while sometimes a high number of post-scandal resignations mitigate a high displacement cost, this was not the case in the 2002 election. Rather, the substantial economic boom in the years leading up to this race prevented an increase in open seats that one might otherwise expect. As Murphy (2003) explains in his overview of the 2002 election:

> For all the government's problems with tribunals and alleged political corruption, by the close of the 28th Dáil it could point to a mass of statistical evidence showing that it had presided over an economic boom. While both Fianna Fáil and the PDs would run as independent parties, it was clear that both would campaign on the government's economic record. (P. 5)

The "natural" decrease in both the presence and value of incumbents in the post-scandal context, therefore, did not materialize, and the displacement cost remained high.

The other high-value variable in the Irish inclusion calculation seems to be the threat cost. Because the norm in Irish candidate selection is to empower the constituency level, the distance between the candidates and the selectors in this system is small. Thus, women's inclusion is a stronger threat to the privileged status of those local-level male selectors than it would be to national-level selectors. For example, in describing how Fianna Fáil determined their candidates, Collins (2003) explains that the national-level committee was involved in selection but followed the lead of the local party organizations in each constituency. The national level of the party, in other words, often acts as a "referee" among the local groups in a constituency rather than a player in the game of candidate selection (Galligan 2003, p. 44). Collins (2003) quotes a party leader in charge of coordinating selection as saying:

> There was a lot of negotiating, a lot of discussion, a lot of argument with the local organizations about the best way to go, the number

of candidates, where they should be from, who they were, who they should be and so on. (P. 23)

The other major party, Fine Gael, used a different method of candidate selection, but maintained the theme of significant localism in the process of selection. Its national-level executive council retains the power to add candidates, but candidates are primarily determined by the local party organization and members (Galligan 2003). Thus, because of the strong role of local-level party elites in candidate selection, an increase in the number of women candidates triggers a substantial threat cost in the inclusion calculus, which in turn decreases the likelihood that elites will select women candidates.

The potential domestic responsiveness benefit of increasing the presence of women in this political context is best described as low, for several reasons. First, the two main parties in the system—Fianna Fáil and Fine Gael—are unlike other parties in Western European systems in that they do not differentiate themselves based on the traditional left/right stances on economic policy or religious involvement in the state. Instead, the left-wing side of the Irish party system is "exceptionally weak" (Coakley 2003, p. 239), and these main parties are both best described as holding relatively center-right ideologies, most similar to Christian Democrat parties in other European countries. Thus, their voters are not likely to reward them for breaking with traditions and modernizing party approaches to gender norms; rather, it is more likely that their voters view gender equality as relatively low on their lists of concerns, though not entirely absent. Further, the patriarchal nature of Irish society during this time—in part due to the strength of the Catholic Church as well as the substantial role of the agricultural and business sectors in the economic system—normalized gender inequality and the more traditional views of women's roles (O'Connor 2008), and thus there was little domestic reward to be found by increasing the presence of women in politics. Finally, while there were women's movements and organizations in this country—such as Irishwomen United—much of their focus was on expanding contraception and abortion access, not on women's political inclusion (Connolly

2002). Thus, there was little mobilization of societal groups around this issue, thereby making elite action on it less likely.

The potential international responsiveness benefit during this period of Irish politics was low as well, largely due to the strained relationship between Ireland and the EU. This relationship is perhaps best described by saying that, were they to declare their relationship status on Facebook, one can be certain that they would both select the "it's complicated" option. There appear to be two main reasons for the complicated nature of this relationship. First, as just discussed, the strong economic growth during the years immediately before the election put the Irish government in a strong and confident position, so there was little strategic need to placate the EU in an effort to facilitate their economic assistance in the short term. Second, issues surrounding increased European integration had been met with much controversy in the legislative session leading up to the election. In 2000, a cabinet minister delivered the famous "Berlin or Boston" speech, in which "she questioned Ireland's role within the EU, argued against closer European integration, and asserted that Ireland had more in common with the United States than with the EU" (Murphy 2003, p. 15). These feelings were not unique to a single minister, but rather her speech reflected general dissatisfaction with the EU and mixed emotions across the government. This was further exacerbated in 2001 when EU finance ministers censured the proposed Irish budget, driving the minister of the economy to declare that "he wouldn't let government fiscal policy be run from Brussels" (Murphy 2003, p. 15). It came as little surprise that the referendum on the EU Treaty of Nice in 2001 was rejected by voters in an election with record low turnout, with a minister of state declaring that even he had voted against ratification (Murphy 2003, p. 16). Thus, the pressures felt by some EU member countries to keep pace with suggested reforms surrounding women's presence in the government were not felt in Ireland; the international responsiveness benefit in this context is therefore best conceptualized as quite limited.

Thus, I argue that, while there would have been an incongruity benefit associated with the inclusion of more women in this political context, the higher displacement and threat costs in this institutional environment prevented this strategic response. That is, because of the candidate-centered electoral system that prizes incumbency, as well as the strong role of local-level elites in candidate selection, the inclusion of women was seen as too costly by party elites. Therefore, one should not expect a post-scandal increase in women candidates in this electoral environment; while the incentive may exist, the inclusion calculus as a whole determines whether women's increased inclusion is a beneficial strategy to elites and, in this case, I argue that it was not.

To examine the effect of massive government scandals on the nomination of women candidates, I collected the candidate lists of Fianna Fáil and Fine Gael parties for the 1997 and 2002 legislative elections.[12] Each data point is the percentage of women on each party list in each district and, as was the case in Spain, there were no legislated gender quotas at the time of either election.

In the post-scandal election of 2002, I argue that the incongruity benefit created an incentive for party elites to run more women candidates than ever before. However, as one would expect due to the other variables in the inclusion calculus, table 4.3 offers evidence that the selectorates of the major parties did not respond to this environment by running more women candidates. Instead, Fianna Fáil actually slightly decreased the number of women running under their party label, and Fine Gael offered

Table 4.3 WOMEN'S PRESENCE IN PARTY LISTS IN IRELAND

Election Year	Party	Average Percentage of Women on Lists (%)
1997	Fianna Fáil	13.20
	Fine Gael	17.50
2002	**Fianna Fáil**	**12.50**
	Fine Gael	**17.45**

NOTE: Election Results in bold occurred in the post-corruption scandal environment.

SOURCE: https://electionsireland.org/results/general/index.cfm.

almost exactly the same number of women candidates as they did in the previous election. Associating the party with women candidates in this context, it seems, came at too high a price.

WOMEN'S DESCRIPTIVE REPRESENTATION IN THE POST-SCANDAL ENVIRONMENT

While the behavior of party elites provides some insight into the effects of an unprecedented corruption meltdown, the voters are an important piece of this argument as well. If there is indeed an incongruity benefit in the post-corruption context, then one should expect voters to be more likely to vote for women in this environment. Further, under most conditions of a massive corruption scandal, the displacement cost decreases because of both the loss of accused incumbents as well as the lower value of incumbency in the post-corruption environment (Klašnja 2015). Thus, the change in the value of these variables should trigger more women to win election to legislative office in the first post-meltdown election. However, it is important to note that, as the case studies illustrated, the nuances of the particular election are critical to determining the other variables in the inclusion calculation; in short, while a corruption scandal increases the incongruity benefit, the institutional and social context of the election determines whether that benefit is "enough" to merit women's increased inclusion.

To analyze the impact of a massive, unprecedented corruption scandal on women's representation, I assembled an original data set of corruption incidents in 17 countries over a time period of approximately 20 years. These 17 countries, listed in table 4.4, were selected from Europe and Latin America and were chosen on the basis of both data availability and democratic status.

To test the validity of my hypotheses, I employed a panel data set and analyzed the relative changes in the percentages of female legislators both before and after massive corruption scandals. In order to capture the effect of women's gains in previous elections, the dependent variable is

Table 4.4 OVERVIEW OF DATA INCLUDED IN REPRESENTATION ANALYSIS

Countries	Years	Average Percentage of Women Legislators (%)
Sweden	1991–2010	44.1
Netherlands	1994–2010	38.3
Finland	1991–2007	37.2
Norway	1993–2009	37.1
Spain	1993–2008	31.3
Argentina	1991–2009	30.8
Costa Rica	1990–2010	29.1
Belgium	1991–2010	28.9
Peru	2002–2011	25.3
Switzerland	1991–2007	24.4
Bolivia	1993–2009	18.1
Italy	1992–2008	15.3
France	1993–2007	13.8
Ireland	1992–2011	13.4
Chile	1993–2009	13.1
Uruguay	1994–2009	12.1
Brazil	1990–2010	7.7

measured using the relative change in the percentage of women in office. For example, in the legislative election in Brazil in 2002, women won 8.6% of the seats. In the following election in 2006, women won 9.0% of the seats. The dependent variable data point for the 2006 election is therefore coded as 0.4%. This, in effect, provides the function of a time lag; that is, this coding accounts for the percentage of women who held office in the previous election.

While there are many available measures of corruption, there are no existing measures that are ideal for this analysis.[13] Thus, I created a new method for measuring both the varying presence, severity, and voter awareness of massive corruption scandals. The data collection was as follows: Using four newspaper databases (Newsbank, Newspaper Source, LexisNexis, and Google News), I performed key word searches for "nepotism," "bribery," "scandal," and/or "corruption" in the news reports of 17 countries over approximately 20 years. I created 14 dummy variables to serve as my measurements of corruption, each designed to pick up variations in the location of the corruption (e.g., was it isolated to a particular branch?), as well as the frequency of the corruption (e.g., were there more than 5 isolated incidents of corruption before the legislative election?), and the type of corruption (e.g., was the corruption a sex scandal?), and coded these variables based on the newspaper articles flagged by the four databases.[14]

By collecting multiple variables on each corruption incident, I can more accurately conceptualize the point at which corruption becomes scandalous. That is, my theory does not address the consequences of systemic corruption, but rather the impact of corruption scandals that decrease the legitimacy of the government. My explanatory variable, therefore, must capture the point at which corruption exits the day-to-day norm and instead becomes a scandal in the eyes of the voters. I therefore measure corruption using a dichotomous variable: if five or more current, national-level political officials in high-ranking positions are publicly accused of an act of corruption, then the variable is coded in the affirmative.[15] In other words, that election is coded as occurring in the midst of a corruption scandal.

In addition, I employ several control variables in this model. Many of these variables have been established in the literature as impacting women's legislative representation, including: the presence of a constitutional or electoral law gender quota (Rule 1987; Tripp and Kang 2008); the number of years since full suffrage was granted to women (Matland and Montgomery 2003; Norris 2004); the average district magnitude of the country (Norris 1985; Rule 1987; Matland and Brown 1992); whether or not the electoral system generates an incentive to cultivate a personal vote (McElroy and Marsh 2010; Thames and Williams 2010; Valdini 2013); and socioeconomic conditions as measured by Gross Domestic Product (GDP) per capita (Inglehart and Norris 2003).[16] In addition, I also include two controls that are more specific to the theoretical core of this project: the first is a dichotomous variable that captures whether there are women involved in the corruption scandal. I suspect that, if women are involved, the positive effect of the corruption scandal for women's representation will be absent or even reversed; the benefit of the stereotype, in this scenario, will be undermined by any women involved in the scandal. Further, I also include a variable to measure the systemic level of corruption in the country. This variable, based on data collected by the Democratic Accountability and Linages Project (Kitschelt 2013), captures the effect of citizens being accustomed to the presence of patron-client relationships or general corruption in government.[17]

Because the data set includes many countries over a 20-year span, I employ a random effects (RE) regression model with robust standard errors. A RE model was selected over a fixed effects model primarily because it allows the inclusion of time-invariant control variables (such as electoral system) and is more generalizable (Bell and Jones 2015). And indeed, a Hausman Test confirmed that the error terms are correlated and thus that the RE model is the appropriate choice.

As table 4.5 displays, when there has been a single massive corruption scandal in the government or multiple, isolated corruption incidents involving high- ranking political elites, there is a significant, positive effect on the legislative representation of women. Specifically, the data suggest that in post-corruption electoral contexts, the relative percentage of women in the legislature increases by about 9% (e.g., if there were 10 women legislators elected in the previous election, there should be 11 women elected in the post-corruption environment). Therefore, there is evidence that the voters respond to massive corruption scandals by increasing their support for women candidates. In addition, while it did not reach conventional levels of significance, there is some evidence that a woman's involvement in the corruption scandal has a negative impact on women's representation. This result is useful, as it suggests a more nuanced response of the voters to a corruption scandal; that is, when the "honest woman" stereotype is vividly contradicted by a woman's involvement in the corruption, voters do not just blindly keep engaging the stereotype. Instead, they respond by limiting their support for women.

Table 4.5 RESULTS FROM RANDOM EFFECTS REGRESSION: EFFECT
OF CORRUPTION ON THE RELATIVE CHANGE IN THE LEGISLATIVE
REPRESENTATION OF WOMEN

Independent Variables	Coefficients
Corruption Scandal	.092**
	(.039)
Women Involved in Scandal	−.063[†]
	(.040)
Gender Quota Law	.037
	(.057)
Average District Magnitude	−.001
	(.001)
Personal Vote	−.055**
	(.033)
Years Since Suffrage	−.003***
	(.001)
GDP Per Capita	−.001
	(.001)
Systemic Corruption	−.051
	(.056)
Constant	1.18

NOTE: $N = 74$; $R^2 = 0.215$; robust standard errors are given in parentheses.

[†] $p \leq .20$, *$p \leq .10$, **$p \leq .05$, ***$p \leq .01$

CONCLUSION

In the eyes of governing party elites, the day that a massive corruption
scandal in the government is exposed is truly the terrible, horrible, no
good, very bad day. This exposure alerts the voters that a party in power—
and perhaps even the party they voted for in the last election—is using
the office for personal gain and thus that this party may not be deserving
of power. These elites, in turn, must focus on damage control; the most
pressing question becomes how to mitigate the scandal such that the electoral fallout is as small as possible. One option is to clean house, change
the norms that led to the massive scandal, and turn over a new leaf with
a focus on transparency, honesty, and a true focus on the good of the

country over the party. This option, however, is unlikely to be chosen—elites have usually benefited from the corruption, perhaps even so much that it affected their previous electoral success, and thus truly removing it is not an optimal path. Instead, in the eyes of these elites, the best move is to *signal* change and *signal* the commitment to honesty and the good of the country, without actually having to take real action on these fronts. The best move, in short, is to push women out in front and let gender stereotypes do the rest.

In this chapter, I examined the effect of a massive corruption scandal on the candidate selection decisions of male elites and found evidence that rational opportunists are usually more likely to run more women candidates in the post-scandal context. In both Spain and Portugal, the revelation of substantial corruption scandals preceded an increase in the presence of women candidates as well as an astounding jump in the number of women positioned at the number one spot on the candidate list. In short, the results suggest that elites saw an advantage to making women the "face of the party" in these post-corruption environments. The case of Ireland, however, illustrated the nuances of elite decision-making surrounding women's inclusion. I argue that the rational opportunist should weigh the costs and benefits of women's inclusion before increasing the presence of women candidates and, in this case, the costs appeared to outweigh the benefits. Due to the value of incumbency and the role of the local-level elites in this system, as well as the limited domestic and international benefit, party elites in Ireland did not respond to massive corruption scandals with an increase in women's descriptive representation. This does not mean that the role incongruity benefit does not exist there, but rather that its potential electoral benefit was not high enough to reconcile the potential costs to elite power. Finally, I examined the effect of revelations of substantial corruption scandals on the voters themselves and found that, perhaps in part due to the presence of more women candidates, more women are elected after massive scandals break. These results suggest that elites often see a strategic advantage to associating their governments or parties with women in the post-corruption context.

In the next chapter, I continue the analysis of elite behavior after a massive corruption scandal, but I focus on a different method of feminizing the party. Another option for elites who see a benefit to women's inclusion—and one that arguably carries a stronger signal—is the adoption of a gender quota that mandates a minimum number of women as candidates. The adoption of a gender quota, I argue, can be a better strategy for rational opportunists than simply increasing the presence of women on the party lists because, depending on the design of the quota, it is potentially easier to limit women's presence and access to power when they are elected via a gender quota. A benefit of this method, in other words, is that it lowers the threat cost of women's inclusion because, if designed carefully, it sends a signal of women's inclusion while simultaneously perpetuating their exclusion.

The Method of Inclusion Matters Too

The Strategy of Gender Quota Adoption

INTRODUCTION

While the previous chapter focused on rational opportunists' perceptions of the costs and benefits of increasing women's inclusion in different contexts, the method of inclusion employed in those analyses—direct and voluntary addition of women candidates to the party lists—is not the only way to increase women's presence. As Matland and Montgomery (2003) explain, there are several different stages in the electoral process at which elites could take action to increase women's inclusion, as well as different methods of inclusion within each stage. For example, in the initial stages of the electoral process—when women are considering the idea of running for office—elites could increase women's presence through a mentoring program. Another option is instituting a gender quota, which might encourage potential women aspirants to give it a go, as well as encourage party leaders to seek out potential women candidates. And in later stages of the process, elites could increase women's inclusion by simply adding them as candidates to the party lists, as I discussed in chapter 4.

In this chapter, I consider the same stimulus but change the method of inclusion, continuing to focus on the impact of a massive scandal but looking beyond candidate selection and voter behavior to consider the adoption of gender quotas. In many ways, the analysis remains the same—this continues to be a discussion of the inclusion calculation of male elites—but the change in method of inclusion allows me to add a necessary layer of complication to the calculation. I argue that the likelihood of increasing women's inclusion is also impacted by the proposed method of doing so; each method has its own specific effect on the values of variables in the inclusion calculation, and thus, the proposed method of inclusion impacts the decision of inclusion. In other words, because each method of inclusion carries a different level of likely presence and power of the newly included women, the question is not simply *whether* to include more women, but *how* to include them as well.

Even though this chapter is narrowly focused on single method of inclusion—the adoption of a gender quota—there is substantial variation in the types of gender quotas available to elites. Most gender quotas require that a specific number of women be included as candidates in the legislative election, but they differ crucially on whether this directive is voluntary or required by law. Voluntary quotas tend to be adopted by a single party at a time and are usually publicized but internal goals for inclusion; there is no explicit penalty for non-compliance, though their voters may get upset if they become aware of a dramatic violation of the quota requirements. Electoral law quotas, on the other hand, require all parties in the country to follow the directive by law and thus usually include a penalty for non-compliance. It is critically important to note that this "penalty" is sometimes so weak that it is effectively meaningless (I will expand on this later as an important consideration of elites when weighing inclusion methods). There are a multitude of other variations in gender quota design, but arguably the other crucial distinction is whether the quota includes a "placement mandate." A placement mandate requires that women be placed in electable positions on party lists, not simply heaped together in the likely unelected bottom of the candidate lists. For example, a quota with a placement mandate will not just say "30% of candidates must be women" but rather "30% of candidates must be women *and* the list positions must alternate between genders." In short, the most important point about gender quotas to remember is that their design strongly impacts their effectiveness and, because of that, one cannot assume that a quota will be effective simply because it exists.

The proliferation of gender quotas in legislatures around the world is remarkable. In a single generation, the quota has gone from an atypical institution adopted only by small leftist parties to being so normalized and mainstream that it is now commonplace to see it in a country's constitution. As of 2018, a majority of countries in the world use some type of gender quota in their legislatures or parties, and these countries are literally all over the map; gender quotas are found in every region, even in countries with very traditional and restrictive views of women's roles.[1] The prevalence and rapid acceptance of this mechanism of inclusion is both fascinating and telling, as it suggests that elites may have found a reason to embrace the gender quota over other possible mechanisms of inclusion.

While it is certainly the case that quotas have spread in part due to women's mobilization, changing international norms, and the transnational sharing of effective methods for women's inclusion, there is also evidence that gender quotas are spreading because of strategic reasons that have little to do with the sincere goal of women's increased representation (Krook 2009). In the next section, I unpack the strategic reasons why the rational opportunist may view gender quotas as the most appealing method of inclusion. I ground my discussion in the existing literature on gender quota adoption, though again I change the lens of analysis to frame the adoption of a gender quota as the result of a rational opportunist's calculation. Specifically, I describe the benefits associated with utilizing a gender quota as the method of inclusion from the perspective of a party or government elite, and consider the conditions under which the gender quota becomes their optimal method of inclusion. In addition, I provide a close case study analysis of gender quota adoption in two countries— Argentina and Italy—and consider the probable reasons why elites found this to be the optimal method of inclusion in these contexts. While there are several nuances in this discussion that prevent it from being absolute, the list of potential benefits gender quotas provide for the rational opportunist is strikingly long; it seems likely that the strategic benefits of quota adoption for existing male elites may be the most powerful factor driving the explosion of gender quotas over the past few decades.

IN THE MIND OF THE RATIONAL OPPORTUNIST: THE POTENTIAL BENEFITS OF A GENDER QUOTA

To unpack the strategic benefits of quota adoption, I offer four general categories of potential benefits of adopting a gender quota from the perspective of the rational opportunist, with a focus on the ways in which this method of inclusion changes the values of variables in the inclusion calculation. First, I examine the unique ability of the gender quota to draw attention, and consider the conditions under which this feature becomes valuable to elites. Next, I examine the effect of the gender quota on creating the perception of tying elites' hands, and suggest that another potential benefit of this mechanism of inclusion is that it conveys a false permanence that increases its usefulness to elites. Then, I consider the impact of the gender quota on the power of male elites, and argue that this method of inclusion can potentially be utilized to sustain and increase their power in multiple ways. This protection of their power occurs when "quota women" are disempowered or marginalized, as well as when the quota serves as a substitute for democratization or decentralization. The final potential benefit of selecting a gender quota as the method of inclusion is, I argue, the most valuable feature of the quota in the mind of the rational opportunist: the ease with which it can be made temporary or ineffective.

Benefit One: Gender Quotas Draw Attention

The first potential benefit of adopting a gender quota as the method of inclusion is the high likelihood that it will draw substantial attention. If one conceives of increasing the presence of women on the party list as gently nudging the voters' perception of the party toward the feminine ideal, then the adoption of a gender quota is akin to grabbing the voters by the shoulders and shouting "WOMAN" in their faces.[2] It is, in other words, the most flashy mechanism of inclusion, which makes it particularly useful if the rational opportunist expects an incongruity benefit to result from women's political presence. For example, if a party sees value in feminizing its reputation in order to signal a commitment to honesty or democracy, adopting a gender quota increases the likelihood that voters (and potential voters) will notice the increased presence of women.

However, while quota adoption can be a very effective maneuver for attracting attention to feminization, it also carries a potential risk of backlash against the party or government that adopts it. There is, for example, the incongruity cost: political parties representing voters who support traditional gender roles could face an electoral penalty for making such a "loud" statement about the inclusion of more women in the public sphere. Parties whose ideology focuses on economic liberalization also face a potential backlash; they will have a difficult time reconciling the mechanism of the gender quota with their stance on the proper level of state intervention in outcomes (Bruhn 2003; Davidson-Schmich 2006; Dubrow 2011). This means, in turn, that this particular mechanism of inclusion will be more costly to elites in conservative and or/economically liberal parties and thus lowers the likelihood that this method will be selected. This is not to say that elites from these parties will never adopt a gender quota, but rather that this mechanism carries a higher cost for them, as it may be in direct opposition to their voters preferences, in a fairly dramatic way.

The conspicuous nature of a gender quota may also be valuable when the rational opportunist expects a substantial domestic or international responsiveness benefit from women's increased presence; a quota offers a simple and public way to signal national and international audiences that progress is being made on women's inclusion. That being said, the type of quota is particularly important here. If the potential international responsiveness benefit is high, then there should be an incentive to adopt a legislated quota or reserved seats. This type of quota affects all political parties, and thus signals that the government as a whole is, for example, associated with the stereotypical inherent democratic behavior of women that the international audience may be looking for. On the other hand, if the domestic responsiveness benefit is substantial, then political party elites have a strong incentive to adopt a voluntary party quota because it only benefits their own party. Existing literature suggests that the adoption of a gender quota is sometimes a strategic attempt to portray the political party as attentive to women's issues and thus garner more votes from women (Norris and Lovenduski 1993; Htun and Jones 2002), so it makes sense that party elites might prefer to limit access to the potential domestic responsiveness benefit. That is, rather than signal that all parties are responding to citizen preferences for increased inclusion, the voluntary quota allows a single party to take the credit, which allows the elites of that party to hoard the potential electoral benefits.

Benefit Two: Gender Quotas Imply Commitment

The second potential benefit of a gender quota as the mechanism of inclusion is the perception that it ties the hands of the party or the state. That is, the fact that this method of inclusion becomes institutionalized—as either an internal political party requirement or as a national law—gives it a level of authenticity and permanence that rises above simply increasing the number of women candidates on the party lists. The gender quota, in other words, carries an implication of sincerity because its institutionalization protects it from the whims of future elites. This method of inclusion, therefore, becomes particularly valuable if the elite is expecting an international responsiveness benefit; in young democracies or hybrid regimes, longevity of reforms is an issue of concern for countries providing foreign aid or building economic relationships, and thus the quota signals a long-term commitment to the ideals that these international figures prioritize (Bush 2011; Bush and Gao 2017). Therefore, because a gender quota theoretically guarantees the presence of women, even if there is elite turnover or some other destabilization of the regime, this method of inclusion creates the impression of perpetuity, thereby creating a higher international responsiveness benefit. In addition, the perception that the hands of the party or government have been tied might also trigger a higher incongruity benefit, especially when the elites see strategic feminization as useful for making the regime appear more democratic to the citizens. By adopting the quota, the rational opportunist signals a permanence to the presence of women, which, as I argued in chapter 3, also signals a permanence to the presence of democracy. The gender quota, therefore, offers the value of perceived perpetuity that cannot be achieved by simply increasing the presence of women on the party lists.

Benefit Three: Gender Quotas Can Protect the Power of Current Male Elites

The third reason why the gender quota could be the preferred method of feminization is that the women elected via a quota are sometimes segregated or disempowered, which in turn lowers the threat cost of inclusion. The work of Franceschet and Piscopo (2008) illustrates this phenomenon in Argentina, where the "quota women" are stereotyped by male legislators as either belonging to a man or simply being crazy ("las locas del 50-50"), which in turn disempowers their ability to pass legislation (p. 420). Bush and Gao (2017) describe a similar situation in Jordan and offer a particularly jarring quote from a former municipal councilor about how the quota women are treated: "Then, when the women councilors try to talk, the men councilors make fun, saying 'Ha, let the quota have her chance to talk'" (p. 154). Webb and Childs (2012) note this phenomenon in the United Kingdom as well, where the hostility and assumptions of poor performance expressed about "quota women" in the Labour Party are generalized to all women politicians of that party, whether or not the quota actually impacted their inclusion. To be clear, I am not suggesting that the thought process of a rational opportunist *explicitly* includes the expectation that quotas will generate a backlash that limits the power and effectiveness of women politicians. It is unreasonable to imagine devilish elites twisting their moustaches and laughing maniacally at their plan to trigger backlash through the adoption of gender quotas. However, it is equally unreasonable to assert that rational opportunists are completely unaware of both the level of cultural acceptance of women's leadership in their country and the typical cultural response to quotas and other affirmative action mechanisms. It seems likely, instead, that most elites have at least a sense of the probable response of both their colleagues and voters to gender quotas and the women who are in office because of them and thus, have a gut feeling as to how much power "quota women" will have access to. Therefore, when there is a low level of cultural acceptance of women's leadership or of the quota mechanism itself, the strategy of inclusion via gender quotas triggers a lower threat cost than in those contexts where women's leadership is more accepted. This mechanism of inclusion, in other words, could be preferred by elites who believe that the potential threat cost of just increasing the presence of women on the candidate lists is too high.

The gender quota may also be the optimal method of inclusion because it can consolidate the power of the party elite. To be clear, this benefit has no direct relationship with women's presence or inclusion; rather, the requirements of the quota sometimes create ancillary benefits which increase party control or even electability. Baldez (2004) notes this phenomenon during the wave of democratization in Latin America. She finds evidence that the pressures to reform and democratize candidate selection procedures caused party leaders to be faced with the choice of either instituting primaries or instituting gender quotas; they chose quotas, because they signal democratic reform without the loss of any real power of the national elites. It seems likely that this (false) association of gender quotas with democratic reform is driven by the stereotypical assumption that women are "naturally" more cooperative, honest, and committed to the ideal of democracy (which I discuss at length in chapter 3). Thus, because of these stereotypes, the incongruity benefit is triggered here, ironically even as actual democracy is being reduced.

The use of this institution to consolidate or increase the power of existing elites has been highlighted by other scholars as well. Weeks (2018) offers evidence that when there is a conflict between the local and national party elites, the adoption of a gender quota allows the national party leadership to exert control over the candidate selection process, thereby undermining the power of the local-level elites without having to explicitly remove their power. In addition, using the case of Jordan, Bush and Gao (2017) find that small tribes improved their electoral representation through the strategic use of reserved seats. This strategy was not driven by an electoral reward for prioritizing gender equality, but rather because the reserved seat design meant that small parties could run women who could "succeed even with the support of relatively few voters" (p. 153). The quota is preferred by these elites, in other words, because its design increases the party's ability to win seats—and thus the elites' hold on power—not because of any benefit associated with women's presence.

Benefit Four: Gender Quotas are Potentially Ineffective and Temporary

Arguably, the most compelling reason why the adoption of a gender quota is an appealing method of inclusion to a rational opportunist is that, while the quota is perceived as institutionalized and sincere, the reality is that gender quotas can be and often are engineered to be temporary or ineffective. Krook (2016) offers evidence of a multitude of ways that elites can resist and subvert a gender quota and emphasizes that "political will" is a crucial (and often missing) ingredient in the successful design and implementation of quotas (p. 268). In her earlier analysis of quota adoption, Krook (2007) specifically references the likelihood that some elites who support quotas are being disingenuous, explaining that:

> empty gestures may embody both a strategy and a counter-strategy for quota adoption and implementation as they facilitate the approval of quotas, but ensure that these policies are unlikely to be applied in line with the broader spirit of the reforms. (P. 377)

Murray (2010) also discusses the tendency of elites to focus more on symbolism than on substance in the creation of quota laws. In her analysis of the parity quota in France—a constitutional amendment requiring that 50% of candidates in each party be women—she notes that:

the weaknesses of the law may well have been intentional, and may have been an integral part of the design of a law that was intended more to please the electorate than to revolutionize the composition of France's political elites. (P. 43)

It seems, therefore, that a rational opportunist who sees a short-term benefit to feminizing the party may see an advantage to adopting quotas over other methods of inclusion due to the potential for undermining the quota; in other words, we should not assume that only compliance is the goal. Instead, the substantial gap between quota policies and quota realities found across systems today suggests that elites may derive benefits from non-compliance and thus may select this method of inclusion because it offers the benefits of attention and institutionalization while being potentially easy to subvert.

If it is indeed the case that rational opportunists view the gender quota as preferable due to the ease with which it can be undermined, then it follows that the elites would also incorporate the likelihood of effective implementation in their calculation of the benefits of women's inclusion. The literature on gender quota implementation includes substantial and often contradictory debates on what factors lead to the successful and complete implementation of a quota, with many scholars coming to the conclusion that this answer is context dependent (e.g., Jones 2009). That is, there are very few ways to guarantee, without a doubt, that a gender quota will be effectively (not) implemented. And yet, while it is impossible to guarantee quota failure, there are circumstances that increase the likelihood that the inclusion generated by the quota will be limited or temporary. In the next section, I discuss three factors that impact the likelihood that the gender quota will be effective: the anticipated response of the high court; the level of ambiguity of the quota law (including the placement mandate and the threshold of representation); and the sanction for non-compliance. These factors, I argue, likely enter into the calculation of a rational opportunist considering the adoption of a gender quota and thus have a substantial impact on whether the quota is selected as the preferred method of inclusion.

While there is scholarly consensus that elites consider the likely response of the high court when deliberating the adoption of a gender quota, there is less consensus regarding the elites' preferred outcome. In her analysis of quota adoption in Mexico, Baldez (2004) frames the motivations of the supporting legislators as sincere; that is, the likelihood that quotas will survive a constitutional challenge increases the likelihood that legislators will choose to pass the quota law. However, following the logic of the rational opportunist theory and the work of Krook (2016), it seems likely that the opposite could also be true. That is, some legislators (elites) do not have a sincere interest in adopting effective gender quotas, and thus the likelihood that a quota law will *not* survive a constitutional challenge should have a positive impact on their passage of the law. In other words, if an elite is looking to send a strong signal of feminization, but is daunted by the threat or displacement costs of women's inclusion, then the knowledge that the high court is likely to overturn the gender quota will increase their willingness to support the law. The gender quota adopted in Italy in 1994 offers an example of this phenomena because, as Guadagnini (2005) explains, most of the legislators who supported the law anticipated that the high court would overturn it (p. 142). However, while a successful court challenge is potentially the best-case scenario for a rational opportunist looking to activate brief benefits of feminization while limiting costs, there is a relatively high level of risk associated with this maneuver. After all, there is no guarantee that the high court will behave as expected, and thus the elite's level of uncertainty regarding the likely response of the court should have an impact on whether this method of inclusion is selected.

Quota design is the second factor impacting the likelihood of successful actualization, and arguably the most crucial design element is the level of ambiguity in the language of the law. Paxton and Hughes (2015) explain that "when the legislated language of a quota leaves room for interpretation, parties may be able to legally meet quota provisions but violate the spirit of quotas" (p. 335). For example, the difference in effectiveness between a law that requires a minimum of 30% women candidates versus a law that requires that *same* minimum with the addition of a placement mandate on the candidate lists is substantial (Jones 2009; Schwindt-Bayer 2009).

A "placement mandate" prevents party elites from placing women at the virtually unelectable spots on the bottom of the list and instead requires that women are given electable list positions. Thus, the presence of an institutional element like a placement mandate may decrease the likelihood that elites would consent to a quota, as its specificity prevents elites from evading the true inclusion of women candidates.

Another important design element is the actual threshold of representation. If the threshold is relatively low, then it may be simple for political parties or governments to meet the quota without changing any of their practices, thereby making the gender quota a much more attractive proposition. In other words, if the quota simply codifies the number of women present in the legislature already, it is unlikely to be seen by elites as carrying high displacement or threat costs. Paxton and Hughes (2017) discuss the trend of quotas that mirror existing representation, noting that in both China and Spain, governments adopted national gender quotas that were virtually identical to women's legislative representation at the time (p. 174). Therefore, it seems reasonable to suggest that, as the difference between the current percentage of women in the party or legislature and the required threshold grows, the less likely a rational opportunist will be to support this mechanism of inclusion.

The final element that should impact whether the rational opportunist supports a gender quota is the likelihood of an effective sanctioning mechanism. Both the presence and effectiveness of enforcement mechanisms vary substantially (Dahlerup and Freidenvall 2005), so one should never assume that a quota will actually be implemented in the way described. France offers a particularly valuable illustration of the impact of sanctioning methods, because different methods were adopted at each level of government. In 2000, France adopted a "parity quota" that required equal numbers of male and female candidates running in all elections. For those elections at the regional level—which used a PR system—the sanction for non-compliance was strong: rejection of the list, which meant that a party that failed to meet the quota would not be allowed to run any candidates in that election. However, for elections to the National Assembly—which used a two-round majoritarian system—the sanction for non-compliance was much weaker: a reduction in state funding which, even if a party refused to run even a single woman, still guaranteed them 50% of their allotted amount (Krook 2009, p. 195). Because of this difference, the rates of quota implementation were dramatically different at the national versus regional level. The sanctioning mechanism, therefore, has a direct impact on whether and to what extent the gender quota will be implemented; if there is a high cost to non-compliance—that is, if the quota has teeth— then the quota is much more likely to be effective (Htun and Jones 2002; Baldez 2004; Schwindt-Bayer 2009). Thus, a quota with teeth should be less appealing to the rational opportunist, because it limits the ability of the elite to sidestep it, even when there is an electoral benefit to doing so. In other words, even if the elite sees a benefit to this selection method for now, a weak enforcement mechanism gives the rational opportunist an "out" if the variables in the inclusion calculation change.

For a rational opportunist, therefore, a gender quota is a method of inclusion that has the potential to bring the benefits of feminization without the costs of shared power, making it a more advantageous option than simply including more women candidates on party lists. While one might initially think of the gender quota as the most sincere or effective way of increasing the number of women in the political sphere, this discussion highlights the many reasons why this inclusion method is potentially ideal for a rational opportunist who is trying to protect his hold on power. It is, in short, false to presume that the presence of a gender quota will have any sort of effect on women or their power, but the symbolism of the quota is so strong that this method of selection triggers the assumption that it will. This may be why gender quotas have become so prevalent; they bring the benefits of theoretically including women while shielding elites from the reality of true inclusion.

GENDER QUOTA ADOPTION IN THE POST-SCANDAL ENVIRONMENT

Here, I offer a close analysis of the adoption of gender quotas shortly after massive corruption scandal revelations in two countries—Italy and

Argentina—and argue that these quotas were adopted as a method of strategic feminization in the context of declining legitimacy. Due to the nature of this analysis, it is impossible to provide direct evidence of the elites' use of the inclusion calculation or of their strategy surrounding the adoption of the gender quota as the method of inclusion. Instead, I offer a discussion of existing literature that suggests that gender quota adoption in both of these cases was driven by elites determining that the benefits of including women—and specifically, their inclusion method of a legislated quota—outweighed the costs. In addition, I also present primary source data in each case study. For Italy, I reference three personal interviews that I conducted with female legislators in the Camera dei Deputati (the lower house of the Italian legislature) in May 2005.[3] For Argentina, I reference the legislative transcripts from the 1991 debate regarding the adoption of a gender quota law in the Cámara de Diputados (the lower house of the Argentine legislature). In both of these case studies, I offer evidence that suggests that elites saw several benefits to signaling an increased association with women—particularly a substantial incongruity benefit—and that the adoption of a gender quota was a savvy method of both activating that signal as well as protecting their own power.

ITALY

Between 1992 and 1994, Italians witnessed hundreds of resignations and arrests of government officials and representatives. Operation "Mani Pulite" ("clean hands"), a massive corruption probe that investigated and subsequently dismantled the Italian government, was in full swing during this period, implicating representatives in every level of government and from almost every party. Many legislators, both local and national, were involved in political scandals so outlandish that they are difficult to comprehend. For example, shortly after the legislative elections of 1992, a government commissioner was forced to take over the city council of Reggio Calabria following the arrests of 25 of its 50 members. The culmination of the clean hands fervor occurred in 1993, when Bettino Craxi, the leader of the Socialist Unity party and a former prime minister, was forced to resign. In that same month, three cabinet ministers resigned under suspicion of corruption, including the minister of justice. Less than four weeks later, two more ministers resigned, pushing the government to the brink of collapse. As Guadagnini (2005) notes, "By the early 1990s, discontent had become crisis. The legitimacy of the political elite collapsed leading to a widespread call for its replacement" (p. 130).

Later that year, an electoral reform referendum was proposed to overhaul the electoral system used in the legislature, which passed with 82.7% of the vote due to citizen frustration with one-party domination, clientelist behavior, and the subsequent corruption that had befallen their system (Palici di Suni 2012). The new electoral system was a majoritarian version of a mixed member system: 75% of the seats were allocated by plurality vote and 25% were allocated by closed-list PR. Shortly after this referendum passed, women representatives in the center-left coalition in the legislature proposed a bill that required the alternation of men and women candidates on party lists—that is, a gender quota—for the seats elected using PR and, after some contentious debate, State Law No. 277/1993 passed (Weeks and Baldez 2015). And thus, in 1994, in the first election after Mani Pulite, a remarkable event occurred: the application of an effective gender quota drove the percentage of women in the Camera dei Deputati from 8.1% to 15.1%.

The passage of this effective gender quota law was surprising, to say the least. While it was clear that a cross-partisan coalition of women in proximity played a strong role in advocating for a quota, why would the male representatives and party leaders allow a bill to be passed that, in the long term, posed a threat to their power? In the discussion that follows, I consider the inclusion calculation variables and argue that the combination of a high incongruity benefit and unusually low displacement and threat costs were particularly instrumental in the elite's decision to support the inclusion of women via a gender quota.

Both the domestic and international responsiveness benefits of women's inclusion appear relatively low during this time and were thus unlikely to have been the primary drivers of this change. It could be argued that women's groups pressured legislators to vote in favor but, as Palici di Suni (2012) notes, "in Italy, due to women's lack of cohesiveness and the technical nature of the issue, [the gender quota] did not receive the same level of visibility or have the same impact as other issues like abortion or sexual violence" (p. 385). Guadagnini (2005) also notes the lack of public concern over women's representation, explaining that, "In the 1990s, the question of women's limited presence in decision-making arenas was still considered by public opinion as a 'women's problem' and not as a question of democracy" (p. 143). There was little mobilization and pressure around this particular policy issue, and thus the domestic responsiveness benefit was likely low. It is also unlikely that an international responsiveness benefit spurred the legislature into adopting the quota, because Italy was not dependent on foreign countries or organizations for aid. And further, at this point in time, the international realm had yet to focus their attention on issues of gender parity, as this quota was adopted before both the UN's Beijing World Conference on Women in 1995 and the EU's Charter of Fundamental Rights of the European Union of 2000. Thus, the international pressure that influenced the inclusion behavior of some EU members—such as Spain and Portugal, as discussed in chapter 4—was unlikely to have been a major factor in this decision.

The incongruity benefit, however, was very high in this environment, and thus strategic feminization became a shrewd strategy; by publicly adopting a gender quota, the government and political parties could cue voters that they were committed to change and following a new path of more honesty and less greed. Paola Manzini, a legislator who was first elected in the post-Mani Pulite election of 1994, explained that some Italian voters were particularly supportive of women because they were seen as symbolizing change. She explained that "part of the electorate is still prejudiced against the role of women in politics . . . but another part of the electorate views women as representing innovation in politics." The experience of Giovanna Melandri, a legislator also elected in 1994 and a member of Prodi's cabinet from 2006 to 2008, also suggests that voters saw women as symbolizing change and, in her case, specifically as a turn away from corruption. In the 1994 election, Melandri's campaign slogan called attention to her gender as well as to the stereotype that women are honest: "parola dei donna"—translated as "the word of the woman." She explained that she chose that slogan because "after the corruption scandals . . . being a woman was something which was useful." In future races, however, her slogans emphasized neither her gender nor any stereotypes about honesty. She explained that "in 1994/95, it [being a woman] was a benefit—I think it's not a benefit anymore . . . women are considered too naïve, they don't exercise power. You need to be harsh and hard-hearted." Melandri, therefore, seemed to see the temporary and contextual nature of the incongruity benefit in that first post-Mani Pulite election and thus ran on a slogan that was specifically designed to activate it. After that election, however, she seemed to see that the incongruity cost would outweigh the benefit of calling attention to her gender and thus avoided it.

The context of Italian politics during this period suggests that the displacement cost of women's increased inclusion was low. The displacement cost is primarily determined by the value of incumbency in that environment and, particularly if there is a high personal vote, this cost can be quite high. And indeed, this cost was quite high in the previous legislative election due to the intraparty preference vote in their former electoral system. But, because of the special circumstances of this election, the displacement cost in 1994 was unusually low. One of those special circumstances was the effect of the Mani Pulite corruption investigation on both the presence and value of incumbents. As Klašnja (2015) explains, corruption scandal revelations can change the blessing of incumbency to a curse, and thus, in addition to the many resignations triggered by the investigation, the value of incumbency itself declined in this environment. The other special circumstance that decreased the displacement cost was that this was the first post-electoral-reform election. In this fluid, post-reform electoral environment, the attachment of legislators to their constituents was in flux; while incumbency still mattered, it did not have the same value as it would in the following elections. Further, one of the explicit goals of the electoral reform was to lower the incentive to cultivate a personal vote, and thus personal traits in the new mixed-member system were less important than in the previous open-list PR system (though, as Giannetti et al. [2014] explain, one should not overestimate the effects of these reforms, as much of the nature of Italian politics remained the same).

In addition, while the specific inclusion method used here—a legislated gender quota—also has the potential to drive up the displacement and threat costs due to the legal requirements of including a specific number of women on candidate lists, it is likely that elites chose this method because they were certain it would not be effective. In other words, this method of inclusion had a negative impact on both the potential threat and displacement costs of increasing the presence of women in the legislature, which made it a savvy choice for elites. Guadagnini (2005) specifically notes that Italian legislators anticipated how the high court would respond to this act and that they passed the quota law because "it was generally held that the provision adopted was likely to be cancelled by the Constitutional Court" (p. 142). And they were right—the quota law was overturned only one year after the election, because, according to the court, the quota infringed on the gender equality provisions in Articles 3 and 51 of the constitution (Guadagnini 2005, p. 141).

This trend of elites in Italy acting to protect their power from the threat of women's inclusion was also raised in my interviews with legislators. All three emphasized that their fates were in the hands of the party leaders more than the voters, and thus, convincing male elites to support them was of more concern than convincing voters. They explained that the party decides both who the candidates are and who gets the resources and the best media exposure, and that the party—even in 2005 and definitely in 1994—was controlled by men. Elena Montecchi, who was first elected to the Camera dei Deputati in 1986 and was thus the most senior of the women I interviewed, was particularly blunt about how the party leadership treated women and why:

> They'll let you get in at the level of deputy, but then there's this barrier—you're not allowed to be in the cabinet or committee chair or other important positions of power. They hinder women, though

my party hinders the least, but it still happens . . . This is because if they assign more positions to women then it takes them away from men. And men know that—they're not fools—they know that if they're relinquishing their power to women then there will be less for them. They're very protective of their power.

The female legislators I interviewed were thus aware that their presence was a threat to male power. Montecchi's description of the male party leaders was not of misogynists delighting in women's oppression but rather rational actors who were protecting their own power by limiting women's access to it. It seems, therefore, that the conceptualization of women's inclusion as a calculation rings true in the case of Italy.

ARGENTINA

As Balán (2011) discusses in his analysis of corruption scandals in Argentina, the years 1989–1991 were exceptional in terms of corruption revelations. By his count, 10 major political scandals came to light during this two-year period, many of which directly involved the sitting president, Carlos Menem. These scandals include the Swift-Armour incident, in which President Menem's brother-in-law demanded a bribe from a US firm in return for a permit to import machinery for a factory in Argentina; the jailing of the National Director of Water Resources on suspicion of laundering drug money; the accusation that the leader of the Peronist block in the lower house of the legislature was involved in multi-million dollar fraud at the state-run petro-chemical plant; and the revelation that Eduardo Menem, leader of the Senate as well as President Menem's younger brother, had a secret and significant bank account in Uruguay stocked with US dollars.[4]

Citizens responded to the revelations of corruption scandals with frustration and dread; not since the "Dirty War" had they seen this level of corruption in government, and they were deeply disturbed by it. In April 1991, a poll revealed that "more than half the population thinks corruption has never been worse and 66% believe Menem's assault on it is only a public relations exercise."[5] Even the Catholic Church expressed dismay: in November of 1990, the president of the National Conference of Catholic Bishops, Monsignor Antonio Quarraccino, stated that that Argentina had become "the paradise of swindlers and opportunists, who take shelter under the rumpled mantle of liberty and democracy."[6] President Menem responded to the growing discontent with constant denials, but also with action, firing countless ministers and advisors in order to shift the blame away from himself and declaring that the new focus of the justice ministry was to spearhead an anti-corruption campaign.[7]

In November 1991, the first legislated gender quota in the world—the *ley de cupos*—passed in the Argentine parliament. The law required that a minimum of 30% of candidates on the party lists be women and that, because they employed a closed-list system to elect their lower house, these women be placed in "proportions which make their election possible" (Jones 1998; Krook 2009). The law passed, according to Krook (2009), "due to combined pressure from women's groups and from then-President Carlos Saúl Menem" (p. 166). The role of President Menem in the passage of this bill is significant: before his intervention, it was widely accepted that the bill would not pass. In fact, legislators were so confident that this bill would fail that the parties didn't even bother to establish an official position for or against the quota (Chama 2001). On the day of the vote, President Menem was alerted that the bill would fail, and thus sent his interior minister to the Cámara de Diputados to instruct the legislators of his party (who held the plurality) to vote in favor of the bill (Krook 2009). The legislators followed his instructions and, to everyone's surprise, the bill passed.

While we will never really know why Menem decided to intervene and ensure the passage of the gender quota law, it seems likely that his support materialized because he realized the potential electoral benefit to being associated with it. Carlos Menem was no angel; he showed no significant interest in women's advancement before this bill. As Krook (2009) describes, "it was an unusual step by Menem who, both before and after the quota law, sided decisively with conservative groups on issues related to women's status" (p. 170). In the following discussion, I consider the inclusion calculation from the perspective of President Menem and argue that his recognition of the particularly high incongruity benefit in this political context was a central reason why he expressed his dramatic, eleventh-hour support for the quota bill. Further, I explain that it seems likely that the displacement, threat, and incongruity costs were relatively low, and that there were potential domestic and international responsiveness benefits to be found. In short, it seems that Menem's inclusion calculation offered a clear result: the benefits of associating himself with an increased presence of women in government outweighed the costs of their inclusion.

Because of the unusually high level of corruption in this political environment, it is likely that President Menem recognized the potential incongruity benefit of associating his government, and more importantly, himself, with the increased presence of women. The expectation that women legislators would be an asset to the state because of their stereotypical communal traits was on full display during the legislative debates of the gender quota bill. Several members of the Cámara de Diputados—including some Peronists—explicitly noted that the quota should be adopted because the presence of more women in the legislature would engender more honesty, kindness, and democracy in the institution. To be clear, I am not suggesting that this was strategic—that is, it is unlikely that Menem supplied these legislators with talking points, particularly because some of them were in opposing parties. Rather, I offer these quotes to demonstrate the power and role of feminine stereotypes in the reaction of both legislators and the public to the gender quota. For example, Sr. Francisco de Durañona y Vedia—a legislator in the Unión del Centro Democrático party, said that he would support the bill because women are more honest than men and, particularly important to the incongruity benefit, he noted that citizens would see them this way as well. He explained:

> I find that women have skills that Argentine society and our institutional organization need today and also that these skills are needed in the renewal that our people are committed to. I think that Argentine women have gifts of heroism and virtue. Women have a predisposition for the concrete and avoid the abstractions that men,

sometimes, lose a lot of time to. They are concrete in the studies they perform and in the way they execute their functions. When there is public outcry against venality and corruption, no citizen imagines a corrupt or venal woman. (P. 4100)[8]

Another legislator, Sra. Ruth Monjardín de Masci of the Partido Federal, echoed this theme, emphasizing her belief that the increased presence of women in the legislature would be an asset due to their natural resistance to corrupt behavior. She noted that:

The woman still does not know or does not participate in the nooks and crannies, the curves or wizardry, which perhaps often their husbands—politicians, businessmen, or workers—resort to in order to gain something in the difficult world of the street. Surely listening to them at the family table the woman's voice will properly say: "Why do you not tell the truth, why do you not do what is right?" That woman is the one I want sitting in this room . . . I believe that this righteousness and that loyalty of the Argentine woman is what we must incorporate into the political and legislative acts. (P. 4120)

Sra. Matilde Quarracino, representing the Partido Demócrata Cristiano, also justified her support for the bill with a reference to feminine stereotypes and the "new style" that women bring to politics. She declared that:

I believe that today more than ever, Argentine society needs the contribution of all its citizens, especially from the feminine world. Thus, through a discourse, a new style and ethics of politics, we will build a much more humane and less cruel world. (P. 4126)

In addition, the explicit association of women with democracy was made by Sr. Carlos Alberto Raimundi of the Unión Cívica Radical party when he stated that:

If the space most conducive to discrimination was the dictatorship, the most conducive space to achieve the equality that we need is democracy.

That is why, furthering this thought, as more women devote themselves to more issues and those issues become even more important, this society will be less discriminatory and more democratic. (P. 4150)

Each of these legislators, therefore, justified their support for adopting a gender quota using feminine stereotypes and specifically noted how being governed by people with these stereotypically feminine behaviors would benefit Argentina. Thus, it seems clear that a central narrative surrounding the quota bill was this idea that women's presence would change things—it would be a "renewal" or a "new style"—in a way based on their stereotypical feminine traits. The popularity of this narrative, in turn, suggests that the incongruity benefit of adopting a gender quota could be substantial in Menem's calculation.

When one is estimating the potential domestic responsiveness benefit of adopting a gender quota, a crucial determinant is the ideological position of the party considering action. Unfortunately, this is difficult to establish in the fragmented and fluid party system in Argentina; Menem was a member of the Peronists—as opposed to the other main ideological identifier in Argentina at this time, the Radicals—and it is challenging to classify these ideologies as more or less left-wing than the other. Voters who identified as Peronist tended to be members of a lower socioeconomic class and/or live in the periphery of the country—and they tended to feel a fierce rivalry with the Radicals—but there was little consistency in the ideological positions and goals of members of these groups (McGuire 1995). However, that being said, the Peronists had taken action on women's inclusion in the past by instituting a voluntary party quota in the early 1950s and the original Peronist, Juan Perón, had been a vocal advocate of granting voting rights to women (Krook 2009). Thus, it seems that Menem could anticipate at least a minimal domestic responsiveness benefit in his inclusion calculation. It is unlikely to be substantial due to his party's fluid ideological positions and fragmentation, but the adoption of a gender quota harkens back enough to his party's glory days that it should trigger at least a minimal benefit among his voters.

The other main determinant of the domestic responsiveness benefit is the level of demand from social movements and/or women's groups in the country. Judging from the descriptions of social movement activity during this time, there was not widespread citizen agitation in support of women's increased inclusion in politics. However, that being said, there was a flurry of activity and awareness cultivated by feminist groups (and legislators, as I will explain momentarily) in the days before the quota bill came to a vote in the Cámara de Diputados. Women came to the capital from all over Argentina and held a "vigil for the quota" in the galleries of the chamber that was so large that it spilled out into the surrounding streets (Krook 2009, p. 169). Thus, while this aspect of the potential domestic responsiveness benefit was not large, it was also not absent; there was enough activist attention on the bill such that supporting it would likely trigger a positive response from the segment of society demanding action.

The potential international responsiveness benefit of adopting a gender quota at this time was unusually high, and thus this may have been a particularly strong variable in Menem's inclusion calculation. In July of 1991, the same year that the gender quota was adopted, the International Monetary Fund (IMF) approved its first "stand-by agreement" with Argentina, which essentially meant that the IMF began loaning Argentina money on the condition of the government undertaking substantial economic reforms. This was the beginning of the (now notorious) Washington Consensus reforms, in which economic advisors affiliated with the IMF and the United States facilitated fiscal reforms such as the Convertibility Plan, which pegged the Argentine currency to the US dollar, as well as liberalized trade, instituted substantial deregulation, and privatized major power and oil industries (Takagi et al. 2004, p. 11). This first stand-by agreement was only to last for one year and then, assuming that the government was following the wishes of the IMF, they would enter into a second agreement—with a much larger loan attached—in early 1992 (Takagi et al. 2004, Appendix 1). President Menem, therefore, had a strong incentive at this moment to signal his commitment to the norms of the organization, as well as to signal that Argentina was moving away from its recent past of economic malfeasance. By adopting a gender quota law, he could do both; by following the growing international norm of gender equality (which was already becoming a priority in the World Bank), he signaled that he was likely to follow the other international norms propagated by the IMF. And further, the adoption of the quota signaled a legislated commitment to women in office, which meant—using assumptions based on gender stereotypes—a more honest, cooperative, and democratic state.

Further, the other variables in the inclusion calculus suggest that this decision would not come with a high cost. The powerful legacy of Eva Perón in Argentina suggests that the incongruity cost of femininizing the government was lower here compared to many other countries in Latin America. Eva Perón—"Evita"—was the First Lady of Argentina from 1946 until her death in 1952. And, while she technically held no official position in the government, it is hard to overstate the importance of her life and legacy in Argentina; for example, as her health began to decline at an unusually young age (she died at 33 of cancer), the Argentine Congress devoted a special legislative session to discussing the fact that she was the "most remarkable women of any historical epoch" and then bestowed a new title on her that had never been given before: Jefa Espiritual de la Nación, which translates to Spiritual Leader of the Nation (Fraser and Navarro 1996, p. 158). Because of Eva Perón's involvement in the political realm reached beyond the role of First Lady—she was a vocal advocate of social welfare issues, for example—part of her legacy is the normalization of women leaders. As Bonder and Nari (1995) explain:

> Eva Perón's power and style have helped to strengthen and legitimize women's presence in politics. She created an idealized model of the "woman politician" which, even today, influences the social and personal expectations of women politicians in Argentina. (P. 184)

Thus, while one should not characterize the incongruity cost in this environment as absent, the legacy of Evita suggests that most constituents would not view women's increased presence in the political realm as unacceptable.

The central determinant of the threat cost is the distance between the elite with primary selection power and the potentially included women.

While previous discussions of this variable have focused on party elite as selectors, similar logic can be applied to the executive decisions on inclusion as well. In a presidential system, the distance between the president and the legislators is maximized; there is a relationship between the president and legislators of his/her own party, but it is nowhere near as intertwined or equalized as that of the prime minister. A prime minister, after all, is usually "first among equals" while the president is separate and distinct from the legislative branch. Thus, from the perspective of President Menem, the women who join the legislature from the gender quota are a limited threat; even if they do gain in power, it will be in a different branch from him and it would take them years to become viable candidates for the presidency. The distance between them, therefore, was substantial and thus the threat cost of inclusion—at least in President Menem's calculation—was low.

While a gender quota has the potential to trigger a high displacement cost, several elements in this context drove that cost down. First, similar to the logic underlying the threat cost in this system, the separation of the executive and legislative branches in a presidential system means that the cost of displacing likely winners in the legislative branch is not as high to a president as it is to a prime minister. This is not to say that it doesn't matter. Presidents would certainly prefer to work with a legislature in which their own party has a majority or plurality. But a prime minister's job depends on it, while the president's does not. Further, at this particular moment in Argentine political history, the relationship between President Menem and the party leadership of his Peronist party was tenuous. From 1989 until about mid-1991, Menem had been following a party-neglecting strategy in which he tended to circumvent his own party in favor of working with the private sector, international actors, and even other political parties (Corrales 2000). Near the end of 1991, this was beginning to change: Menem was now engaging a strategy of party accommodation, and even declared that he was "feeling more Peronist than ever before" (Corrales 2000, p. 136). This suggests that when considering the adoption of a gender quota at the end of 1991, President Menem was likely more invested in the legislative fate of the party than before, but that this relationship was not yet strong. In fact, at this moment in time, the gulf was only beginning to heal. Thus, because of the separation between the president and his party, Menem's inclusion calculation likely included a lower displacement cost of adopting a legislative gender quota. Another key determinant of the displacement cost is the legislative electoral system. The Cámara de Diputados employed closed list PR system and thus, because this type of system generates a low incentive to cultivate a personal vote, the loss of male incumbents would not trigger a substantial electoral cost for the party. Finally, the method of inclusion itself—the gender quota—lowered the potential displacement and threat costs because the final version of the bill that passed did not include a placement mandate. As Krook (2009) explains, there was instead a vague statement that these women should be on the list "in proportions which make their election possible," but no one could agree how to interpret this and thus President Menem issued a decree to clarify it in 1993 (p. 170). But at the point of passage, the bill was vague enough that the voting legislators likely noticed the sizable loophole that would be present in the gender quota law, and this increased their comfort with supporting the law.

Because women are different from one another and, even when they agree, tend to have little access to power, the effect of women in proximity cannot be predicted in a systematic way and is thus not a variable in the inclusion calculation. That being said, the women in proximity in Argentina at this time had an important and positive effect on the adoption of this gender quota. Women in both the Peronist and Radical parties began advocating for a quota in the 1980s, and a female senator from the Radical party, Margarita Malharro de Torres, was the first to submit a gender quota bill in the Senate in 1989. Shortly thereafter, a group of female legislators in the Cámara de Diputados also introduced a quota bill and found cross-party support among women. Most men, however, did not support the bill, but were willing to pass it because "most senators were certain that the bill would be rejected or would expire before it could be addressed in the Chamber of Deputies" (Krook 2009, p. 168). Once it passed, these women in proximity directed media attention toward the bill and mobilized women around the country to contact their legislators and request support for the bill (Krook 2009), thereby generating a large potential domestic responsiveness benefit to its adoption.

While it is impossible to truly know what inspired President Menem to intervene and save this law from defeat, this discussion of the potential costs and benefits of adopting a legislative gender quota suggests that he foresaw a strategic advantage from facilitating its passage. By being responsible for an institutionalized association of his party—and most importantly, himself—with women, President Menem countered the corruption narrative with a signal of reform, change, and a new embrace of honesty and inclusion. Thus, without making any substantive changes at all in his political practices, he gave the impression that his regime would be less corrupt in the future. Further, from his perspective, the displacement, threat, and incongruity costs of increased women's inclusion were low, and the potential international and domestic responsiveness benefits that he could cultivate from this action were relatively high. In short, the question of whether to facilitate the adoption of a gender quota law at this moment in Argentina was, from his perspective as a rational opportunist, an easy one.

CONCLUSION

The dramatic increase in the adoption of gender quotas by governments and political parties during the past few decades could be interpreted as evidence that there are indeed angels among us. It could be that the men who advocated for and facilitated these quotas decided that justice and equality matter more than maintaining their own personal power and are thus selflessly dismantling the patriarchy and replacing themselves with women. While this is possible, it is unlikely. More likely is the possibility that the proliferation of gender quotas across the world is due, at least in part, to the benefits of this particular method of inclusion to men in power.

In this chapter, I examined the potential benefits of a gender quota from the perspective of male elites, and found several different ways that this institution could be the perfect balance of both feminizing the image of the party or government while simultaneously restricting women's presence and power. I argued that this method of inclusion is an excellent tool for signaling domestic and international audiences; it both draws attention to the theoretical feminization—and thus potential incongruity benefit—and signals credibility and commitment due to its institutionalization. Further, the gender quota can also be used as a savvy tool for consolidating the power of party elites, because it places more control into the hands of leaders while ironically giving constituents the impression that democratization is occurring. Finally, and arguably most importantly, a gender quota may offer these benefits while simultaneously limiting both the power and presence of women, thereby making it a very attractive method of "inclusion" in the eyes of a rational opportunist. The gender quota can restrict women's power in those environments where women elected via quota are viewed as ineffective or crazy (e.g., "las locas del 50-50"), and can limit women's presence through a careful design that makes it either likely to be overturned by the high court or vague enough to be easily ignored. In the case analyses of Italy and Argentina presented in this chapter, I offered evidence that elites adopted a gender quota in each of these countries because they saw a potential political benefit from associating their governments with women in the post-scandal context. Their inclusion calculations, in other words, demonstrated an overall benefit to increasing women's presence and, thanks to the unique advantages of the gender quota mechanism, this particular tool both maximized those benefits while minimizing the costs.

In the next chapter, I turn away from the stimulus of corruption scandal revelations to consider the inclusion calculation in the context of a hybrid regime with declining levels of democracy. Because leaders in a hybrid regime are attempting to maintain a pseudodemocracy, a loss in civil rights or a removal of democratic procedures must be countered with something that replaces that lost democratic legitimacy. That something, I argue, is the increased presence of women in the legislature or, as I discuss in my case studies of Bangladesh and Ethiopia, the adoption of a gender quota.

The Strategic Use of Women's Representation in Hybrid Regimes

INTRODUCTION

If women's presence in public office can be used strategically to signal certain traits about the government, then there is little reason to expect this effect to be limited to democracies. In this chapter, I suggest that non-democracies can strategically increase the presence of women in government so as to trigger their citizens to associate honesty, cooperation, and democracy with the government. But, as in democracies, this association is not always beneficial to the government, and thus there are only certain contexts in which stereotypically feminine traits gain enough value to merit women's inclusion. I argue that one of those contexts is the loss of democratic traits in a hybrid regime: in this scenario, as a government shifts away from democracy by removing civil rights or changing electoral law, there is an incentive to simultaneously increase the presence of women in the legislature or adopt a gender quota so as to signal the citizens that the government still maintains democratic traits. I examine this theory using a cross-sectional time series model that utilizes the election results of 27 countries over 16 years. Further, I present case studies of Ethiopia and Bangladesh, two hybrid regimes that experienced a dramatic reduction in civil rights while simultaneously adopting gender quotas and increasing the presence of women in politics. My results suggest that, when a hybrid regime becomes less democratic, there is an incentive for rational opportunists to increase the descriptive representation of women. I argue that these results suggest that government elites may be using women's representation as a strategic tool in an effort to mimic a democracy.

WOMEN'S ROLE IN CULTIVATING LEGITIMACY IN NON-DEMOCRACIES

In recent decades, the association between women's representation and democracy has increased in popularity as more and more international organizations, scholars, and states declared the inclusion of women to be a key element of a well-functioning democracy. As discussed in chapter 3, the initial point that women *should* be included in democratic governments has since transformed into an *if/then* mythology— that is, *if* there are significant numbers of women in the government *then* the government is, or is more likely to be, a democracy. This transformed conception is fundamentally incorrect due to its reliance on stereotypes and an essentialist view of women, yet this reality does not seem to be interfering with its popularity. Instead, women's presence in a government is a widely accepted signal—both domestically and internationally—that the government is embracing at least some democratic principles.

Because of this association, non-democracies can use women's descriptive representation as a substitute for true democratic activity, thereby triggering the international and domestic benefits of a supposed increase in democracy without elites having to actually sacrifice any power. In other words, the potential incongruity and international responsiveness benefits from women's inclusion are high in this regime type. That being said, women's increased inclusion is not necessarily a good strategy in all non-democracies; the inclusion calculation will differ across states and, because many authoritarian regimes rest at least part of their legitimacy on presenting a hyper-masculine image of the state and its leaders (e.g., Russia, as Sperling [2015] points out), the prospect of feminization by association is not necessarily desirable. Further, just as some non-democracies might not want to signal feminization, others may not want to signal any embrace or welcoming of democratic reforms, preferring instead to present the government as fully and completely in control of itself and the state.

One particular type of non-democracy, however, performs a unique balancing act between authoritarianism and democracy: the hybrid regime. As Diamond (2002) notes, there has been an unprecedented increase in the number of pseudodemocracies or hybrid regimes during the past few decades. This type of regime is neither purely democratic nor purely authoritarian; it has some traits of democracy (such as a constitutional requirement to hold elections on a regular basis) but also has characteristics of authoritarianism (such as restricting voting rights or freedom of the press). In a pseudodemocracy, governments do not go about maintaining power in blatant and obvious ways—these are not the traditional totalitarian regimes of years past that brazenly and proudly trumpeted their unilateral power. Instead, they cultivate a level of legitimacy by maintaining some characteristics of a democracy, and thus benefit from their citizens believing that there is some degree of openness, inclusivity, and freedom in the regime. There is, however, an obvious counter-incentive to making the regime truly more open, inclusive, and free: it increases the likelihood that the opposition will successfully unseat the government. The pseudodemocracy, therefore, lurks in the grey area of governance, and with good reason: Diamond (2002) argues that in the contemporary era, "democracy is the only broadly legitimate regime form, and regimes have felt unprecedented pressure (international and domestic) to adopt—or at least to mimic—the democratic form" (p. 24).

Being able to mimic the traits of a democracy without actually becoming more democratic is therefore of the utmost importance in a hybrid regime. The regime gains legitimacy when citizens believe that their voices matter (Weber 1946); little can be gained from a government in a hybrid regime being brash and obvious about the limits of citizen control. Thus, because this is not a fully authoritarian regime, the government must prioritize low-risk strategies for signaling democracy (or even allowing it at low levels) without allowing a transition to an actual democracy. There are obvious ways that a hybrid regime could do this—for example, by holding elections that the government refers to as free and fair while simultaneously oppressing the voting rights of certain groups, or by removing punishments against journalists and thus creating a technically free press while simultaneously bribing or prioritizing only the news agencies that report favorably about the government. However, the problem with these methods and many others like them is that they carry significant risks; that is, either of these paths could potentially give the impression of democratic competition without the likelihood of having to sacrifice power, but they (and many other strategies like them) require intense coordination which could easily be undermined or fall short. It seems clear, therefore that pseudodemocracies are always on the lookout for simple and low-risk ways of signaling a democracy without actually becoming one.

Because of the pressure to "mimic" a democracy in hybrid regimes, I argue that the incongruity benefit—that is, the positive signal sent by women's presence in government—is particularly valuable in this context, and not just as a signal to potential foreign aid donors. The adoption of a gender quota or the inclusion of more women in the legislature is a low-cost, low-risk maneuver that sacrifices no real power yet presents the image of power resting in the hands of citizens. That is, because of the stereotypes associated with women, an increase in the presence of women in government serves as an information shortcut suggesting increased democracy. And, unlike democracies, non-democracies have at least some ability to manipulate electoral outcomes, and so their governments can strategically add more women to the legislature if they decide to do so; they are not as beholden to the whims of the voters, and can thus respond more easily and quickly to potentially beneficial contexts. In short, pseudodemocracies have the motive and the method to strategically feminize the government.

CROSS-NATIONAL ANALYSIS

If, as I argue, governments in hybrid regimes strategically manipulate women's representation in an effort to mimic democracy and therefore cultivate legitimacy, then this behavior should be most visible after a change in the level of civil and political rights. When the government in a hybrid regime increases the restrictions on media, or alters the voting rules in an effort to exclude opposition forces, their legitimacy takes a direct hit; the hybrid regime leaves the grey area of governance as it becomes more clear that the regime is taking steps to actively subdue and avoid the will of the people. The break in the status quo, therefore, forces the hybrid regime to take steps to cultivate legitimacy and, as I have argued, the addition of women to the legislature is a simple way to give citizens the impression of a more democratic state without actually having to behave as one. Based on these ideas, I offer the following hypothesis: As the level of democracy decreases in a hybrid regime, there is a positive effect on women's descriptive representation in the legislature. In the following discussion, I test this hypothesis using an original data set of women's legislative representation in 27 countries in the time period 1999–2015.

Table 6.1 lists the countries included in the data set. The level of democracy in each of these regimes is captured using the Polity2 score, a composite measure of the level of democracy/autocracy of a state based on such indicators as the regulation and competitiveness of voter participation and the constraints on the chief executive.[1] The Polity2 scale ranges from –10, applied to states considered to have maximum levels of authoritarian traits (e.g., North Korea), to +10 for states with maximum levels of democratic traits (e.g., Australia). A score of 0 means that a state is equally authoritarian and democratic—the very definition of a hybrid regime. Thus, I included in my analysis only those countries with average Polity2 score between –5 to +5 due to the emphasis on the strategic motivations of hybrid regimes in my theory; elites in a country scoring in the –5 to +5 range are likely to have the incentive to mimic democratic traits but not the desire to transition to a democracy. Further, I excluded all states with

Table 6.1 OVERVIEW OF HYBRID REGIME DATA SET

Country	Election Years	Average Percentage of Women Legislators (%)	Average Polity 2 Score
Algeria	2002–2012	15.00	0.33
Angola	2008–2012	36.35	−2.00
Armenia	1999–2012	6.90	5.00
Bangladesh	2001–2014	13.53	0.33
Burkina Faso	2002–2015	13.08	1.20
Cambodia	2003–2013	15.47	2.00
Central African Republic	2005–2011	11.75	−1.00
Chad	2002–2011	10.05	−2.00
Dem. Rep. of Congo (Kinshasa)	2006–2011	8.65	5.00
Egypt	2000–2015	5.28	−3.75
Ethiopia	2000–2015	23.93	−2.00
Haiti	2000–2015	2.55	0.75
Ivory Coast/Côte d'Ivoire	2000–2011	9.75	4.00
Jordan	2003–2013	8.73	−2.75
Liberia	2005–2011	11.05	5.00
Malaysia	1999–2013	10.18	4.50
Mozambique	1999–2014	35.90	5.00
Nigeria	2003–2015	4.95	4.75
Papua New Guinea	2002–2012	1.50	4.33
Russia	1999–2011	11.28	4.25
Rwanda	2003–2013	56.30	−3.00
Sri Lanka	2000–2015	4.70	5.00
Tajikistan	2000–2015	17.05	−2.50
Tanzania	2000–2015	31.10	0.00
Tunisia	1999–2014	23.98	0.00
Togo	1999–2013	9.63	−2.50
Zambia	2001–2011	12.53	5.00

populations of less than one million due to the challenges of gathering control variable data in very small countries.

The model used here incorporates several control variables to capture the effects of other factors deemed predictive of women's legislative representation. While most of these variables have been tested primarily in the context of democracies, there is a chance that they could impact representation in hybrid regimes as well, and thus I include them here. From the category of structural predictors that may impact the supply of candidates, I include the literacy rate of women citizens in the election year, as well as the GDP per capita. I also include three institutional variables that are often found to be important predictors of women's representation: the presence of legislated gender quotas; the number of years since women's suffrage was attained; and the use of a PR system to elect the legislature. In addition, based on the research of Moghadam (2003) and Charrad (2011) on the effect of Sharia law on women's representation in non-democracies, I include the percentage of citizens practicing Islam. The model also includes two variables to measure the impact of conflict: the presence and level of civil violence and/or warfare during the election year; and a dichotomous variable that captures whether civil conflict concluded during the years preceding the election. As discussed in chapter 2, the end of conflict has been found to have a positive effect on women's representation (Hughes 2009; Hughes and Tripp 2015), which I attribute to the lower displacement and incongruity costs, as well as the increased international responsiveness benefit. Finally, to specifically address the pressure and potential benefit of international responsiveness, I include a measure of international aid received by the country: the net official development assistance (ODA) received as a percentage of gross national income.[2]

To model this relationship, I use the *change* in the Polity2 score from the previous election as my primary independent variable. For example, the Polity2 score in Ethiopia at the 2000 legislative election was +1, but it decreased to –3 at the 2005 election. Thus, the year 2005 is given the score of –4 because of the decrease in 4 points since the previous election. As my primary dependent variable, I use *relative change* in women's legislative representation. I measure representation based on the relative change in the percentage of women legislators (not aggregate), because it may not be reasonable to expect the effect of the loss of democracy to be universal but rather relative to a previous level of representation. In other words, if the number of women legislators increased by 4%, this change would be quite noteworthy in Zambia (due to their low level of women's representation) but less so in Tunisia. Thus, each data point of the dependent variable is calculated by first determining the change in women's representation from one election (T-1) to the next (T-2) and then dividing it by the aggregate percentage of women at T-1. For example, the percentage of women in the Ethiopian lower house in 2000 was 7.7%. In 2005, however, it grew to 21.4%. Thus, the data point for the year 2005 is 13.7/7.7, which equals a relative change of 178%. Finally, because this is a panel data set with both a cross-sectional and time-series dimension, I use a random effects model clustered by country.[3,4]

The results shown in table 6.2 offer evidence that, as I posit, political elites strategically use women's representation to signal democracy and inclusion. When the level of democracy increases from one election to the next, there is a significant, negative effect on women's presence in the legislature. For example, if a regime restores enough civil rights to score a 2-point increase in Polity2, then the relative percentage of women in the legislature decreases by about 34%.[5] However, if a country removes civil rights and scores a 3-point decrease in their Polity2 score, the relative percentage of women in the lower house will increase by 51%. In other words, if there were 10 women in the legislature and a country removes enough of their democratic behaviors to fall by 3 points on the Polity2 scale, then there are, on average, 15 women "elected" at the next legislative election. These results also suggest that the effect of legislated gender quotas on women's representation is significant and positive, as is the conclusion of civil conflict, which further supports the findings of Hughes (2008) and Hughes and Tripp (2015) . Finally, religiosity has a small but significant effect, though in an unexpected direction: as the percentage of people who identify as Muslim increases, there is also a small increase in the relative change in women's representation.

Table 6.2 Results from Time-Series, Random Effects
Regression: Effect of Change in Level of Democracy
in Hybrid Regimes on the Relative Change in Women's
Representation

Independent Variable	Coefficient
Change in Level of Democracy (Polity2)	−.17*** (.04)
Gender Quota Law	.72** (.35)
Proportional Representation	−.24 (.27)
Women's Literacy	−.01 (.01)
Civil Conflict	−.02 (.09)
Conclusion of Civil Conflict	.86** (.35)
Foreign Aid Received	−.00 (.01)
Percentage of Practicing Muslims	.009** (.003)
Years Since Women's Suffrage	.01 (.01)
GDP per capita	.00 (.00)
Constant	.46

NOTE: $N = 91$ R^2: Within = .25. Between = .54. Overall = .32.
Figures in parentheses are standard errors.

*$p \leq .10$, **$p \leq .05$, ***$p \leq .01$

While the results of this analysis suggest a correlation between the decline of democratic traits in a hybrid regime and women's political presence, this is not enough to successfully make the case for causation. Thus, in continuing this analysis, I present case studies of two hybrid regimes: Ethiopia and Bangladesh. These countries were selected as case studies for several reasons. First, they are in many ways "typical" cases that should exemplify the relationship just examined. Second, they vary in the severity and speed of loss of democracy. In Ethiopia, the decline in democratic characteristics was a slow burn, with freedoms quietly chipped away and power centralized over several years. In Bangladesh, on the other hand, the decline in democratic traits was sudden and dramatic: its Polity2 score decreased from +6 for the 2001 election to −6 for the subsequent 2008 election. This variation, therefore, allows further insight into whether the magnitude of the democratic loss affects the likelihood that political parties turn to women to increase their legitimacy. Finally, Ethiopia and Bangladesh were chosen because of the differences in the primary religion of the majority of their citizens. As discussed earlier, the use of Sharia law has been shown to have a negative effect on women's representation in non-democracies (Moghadam 2003; Charrad 2011). However, this variable did not have the expected impact in the regression model used in this analysis, which suggests that either the presence of Islam in society was measured poorly or that—as the model suggests—it does not seem to matter in this particular political context. By offering a case study of a country in which a vast majority of people who identify as Muslim—Bangladesh—as well as a study of a country with a small, minority population of people who identify as Muslim—Ethiopia—one can gather further insight into the effect of this variable under conditions of declining democratic behaviors.

ETHIOPIA

In 1991, the Ethiopian People's Revolutionary Democratic Front (EPRDF) and the Tigray People's Liberation Front (TPLF) joined together to end the 17-year civil war and remove power from the military regime. Shortly after, the EPRDF completely restructured Ethiopian politics and society using the homegrown ideology of "revolutionary democracy" as the regime's basis (Bach 2011). This ideology, while self-described as "revolutionary" and "democracy," actually fits the definition of a classic pseudodemocracy: the government is unwilling to share power, the judicial branch is very weak, and the government actively oppresses civil rights and the media. Thus, while the citizens were initially hopeful about the democratic prospects for their country, the reforms and electoral restrictions implemented during the 1990s revealed to them that their government had no sincere interests in decentralizing power. Here, I argue that the loss of legitimacy due to the failed promise of democracy drove the EPRDF to increase the presence of women in the legislature. The government was clearly concerned about their domestic legitimacy and international responsiveness during these years and thus viewed women's association with democracy as a valuable tool; rather than make substantive changes that would have threatened their power, they were able to mimic democratization simply by emphasizing their adoption of a gender quota and dramatically increasing the presence of women in the legislature.

There is substantial evidence that the EPRDF government was concerned about cultivating and maintaining its domestic legitimacy and yet did not choose to cultivate this legitimacy by increasing the level of democratization in their country. For example, the adoption of a system of ethnic federalism, which even included a provision in the 1995 constitution that referred to a "right of secession from the federation," demonstrates that the government was actively trying to gain favor with the highly ethnically and linguistically diverse population. As noted by Riedl and Dickovick (2014) in their analysis of Ethiopia:

> in many instances where regimes have once confronted fundamental challenges to central legitimacy, decentralization becomes an adaptive strategy that enables regime maintenance and entrenchment. (P. 340)

However, while the 1995 constitution initially appeared to establish more regional independence, citizens slowly began to realize that this impression was false. The legislative elections held in 1995 and again in 2000 were essentially non-competitive, as evidenced by the EPRDF and its surrogate parties winning more that 90% of the seats (Gudina 2011). This clash between the reality of governance and the ideals presented in the constitution perhaps became most clear in 2003, when the legislature gave the central government the power to directly intervene in regions when they thought there was a deterioration in the security (Abbink 2006). Thus, as the promise of increased independence and democracy proved untrue, the government had to cultivate other methods for maintaining its legitimacy. After all, as Hagmann and Abbink (2011) explain, "much of the EPRDF's credibility, political identity, and claims to legitimacy to rule draw on the purported democratization, modernization, citizens' inclusion, and development of the country" (p. 583). In short, the party had to do something to counter the perception of lost democracy or risk the end of its regime.

As the 2005 election approached, a shift in the EPRDF's strategy became clear: perform democracy. Some non-democratic restrictions remained, such as the prohibition on local NGOs as election observers, but unprecedented freedoms were granted to opposition parties and state-run media (Abbink 2006). It was, in the words of one journalist, an "exceptional" time in terms of media freedom and neutrality (Stremlau 2013, p. 126). However, while citizens initially believed these changes were sincere steps toward democratization, scholars have not found any evidence of sincerity. Instead, as Aalen and Tronvoll (2009) explain:

> In retrospect, it is apparent that the EPRDF had not expected that the liberalization ahead of the 2005 elections would entail any real challenge to its position, but instead had calculated that it could keep control in its own hands at the same time as profiting from an enhanced democratic image. The elections were thus seen as tools not for enhancing democracy in Ethiopia, but for consolidating EPRDF's power. (P. 196)

Under these circumstances, the incongruity benefit in the inclusion calculation was quite high; the EPRDF was quickly losing legitimacy as citizens realized the reforms were false, and thus women legislators could be used as a substitute for the promised democracy. And, judging from the actions of EPRDF elites, this is exactly the path they chose. In previous years, women's presence in government had not been of any concern for the party—which is clearly reflected in the legislative election results of 2000 when women won 7.7% of the seats—but in 2004, the party adopted a voluntary gender quota which required that 30% of the candidates be women. Shortly afterward, the EPRDF was explicit about their desire to associate women legislators with democracy: for example, the vice-chairwoman of the Women's Affairs Standing Committee in Parliament declared that "for the country to be a true democracy, women must be properly represented."[6] The quota proved to be quite effective: the number of women in the legislature nearly tripled, with an unprecedented jump to 21.4% of seats held by women after the 2005 election. The presence of women continued to rise, and after the 2015 election, Ethiopia ranked number 16 in the world for women's representation with 39% of the legislative seats held by women.[7]

While it is possible that this unprecedented rise in women's presence in the legislature could have been driven by a commitment by the voters to elect women candidates, there are four factors that suggest that these results were instead the product of a strategic decision by EPRDF elites. First, there was substantial evidence that the National Electoral Board of Ethiopia (NEBE) manipulated the 2005 vote results in favor of the ruling party. The results of 299 districts were officially disputed by the opposition parties, media, and foreign observers, yet the NEBE only allowed new elections in 39 of those districts, following which several high-ranking but unpopular regime leaders who were defeated in the first election were returned to office (Abbink 2006). Second, even if one questions the extent of their ability to rig the election, the presence and power of local networks of party control suggests that the EPRDF strongly impacted voter behavior. These local networks were intricate and effective mechanisms for cultivating intense patron-client relationships between the voters and the party; as Aalen and Tronvoll (2009) explain, "voters understood that if they did not vote for the ruling party they would lose access to social services and other benefits provided by the kebale (local neighborhood administration)" (p. 197). Thus, from a logistical perspective, the EPRDF had the mechanisms in place to artificially increase the number of women in office. Third, the fact that the party voluntarily adopted a gender quota that would only apply to itself—rather than a legislated quota that would apply to all parties—suggests that it saw a strategic benefit to associating only the EPRDF with women's inclusion. If this was a sincere response to a growing public agitation for women's equality, the EPRDF would have most likely chosen a legislated gender quota so as to force all parties to bear the weight of the higher incongruity cost that would result from women's inclusion. Finally, the unprecedented number of women legislators was achieved via a single-member district electoral system which, to say the least, is an unusual result for this type of electoral system. One of the most well-known and accepted theories in the study of gender and electoral systems is that, when compared to proportional systems, majoritarian electoral systems such as this have a powerful negative effect on the representation of women in legislatures (Rule 1981;1987; Norris 1985; Matland 1993; Darcy, et al. 1994; Matland and Studlar 1996). Thus, it is very unlikely that substantial numbers of women would be "naturally" elected under these electoral rules, particularly with such quick jumps in their representation. The fact that they were, therefore, suggests some sort of intervention in the result. Thus, it seems likely that the party elites strategically increased the presence of EPRDF women both before and during the 2005 legislative election in an attempt to curtail their loss of legitimacy from increased authoritarian behaviors.

In addition to the legitimacy cultivated through the role incongruity benefit, there is also a potential international responsiveness benefit from women's inclusion in Ethiopia. As predicted by Bush (2011) and Paxton and Hughes (2017), the promise of increased foreign aid resulting from the increased presence of women in politics was a powerful driver. Shortly after the EPRDF transition to power, Prime Minister Meles made a commitment to Western countries granting aid—of close to 2 billion U.S. dollars a year—that he would "guarantee the right of political parties to compete on a level ground" (Milkias 2011, p. 92). However, as it became clearer over time that Ethiopia was in fact receding from its democratic claims, the government had to act in order to protect its foreign aid allotment. Thus, the potential international responsiveness benefit of women's inclusion was substantial. That being said, it is also important to note the recent changes in the donor community that may be decreasing the international responsiveness benefit. In recent years, China cultivated strong economic ties with Ethiopia and became an important source of foreign aid, and the Chinese have made it clear that their greatest concern is economic growth, not democracy nor human rights (Hagmann and Abbink 2011). Thus, while this variable was certainly an important part of the inclusion calculation, it is likely not the only driver of the increase in women's legislative presence.

In addition to these benefits, the costs of women's inclusion were relatively low during this period. For example, under normal circumstances, the displacement cost in this type of institutional environment would be substantial due to the use of the single-member district electoral system. However, because this election was not free and fair and was—at the very least—deeply affected by the patron-client relationship connection between the EPRDF and the voters, the displacement cost was actually quite low. There was little penalty for removing incumbents and replacing them with women because, as discussed by Aalen and Tronvoll (2009), the extensive neighborhood network of clientelism functioned to keep voters loyal to the party, not a particular legislator. In addition, the threat cost is also low in this system. The distance between the inclusion point—that is, the addition of women candidates—and the party elites was substantial; thanks to the heavily centralized structure of the party and tight control of the local-level networks, EPRDF could virtually guarantee that the vast majority of legislators would have little access to the true power in the party. That is, while the federal system and presence of neighborhood administration may have appeared to decentralize power, they "in fact acted as a mechanism for reinforcing central control through the party structure" (Gudina 2011, p. 667). Finally, again due to the tight control of the election outcome—via either direct election rigging and/or the clientelist system that engineered a strong connection to the EPRDF—one can also assume that the incongruity cost was low in this system. While many voters may have felt some discomfort with women legislators, this issue would be overcome for most by their desire to maintain the benefits they receive from being loyal to the party. Thus, it seems likely that the threat, displacement, and incongruity costs of women's inclusion were low.

Without a doubt, the self-described revolutionary democracy of the EPRDF regime saw a value in mimicking the traits of a democracy without actually becoming one. But as citizens realized that the party's embrace of democracy was simply a performance—particularly after the noncompetitive elections of 1995 and 2000—the EPRDF had to offer them new evidence that it was still committed to the idea of democracy. Women's inclusion, therefore, was a strategic tool used because of women's stereotypical association with democracy; their increased presence was strategically employed to signal the citizens that the government continued to have some sort of attachment to democratic ideals even though, in reality, its commitment to democracy was fading away.

BANGLADESH

Since gaining its independence from Pakistan in 1971, Bangladesh has endured multiple military coups and political assassinations as well as general instability. While the country was able to transition away from military rule and toward democracy in 1991, it was far from consolidated: extreme clientelism, a venomous dynamic between the two major parties, and slow but steady increases in political violence and religious militancy consistently undermined the country's stability. And after the 2001 election, Bangladesh took a dramatic shift away from democracy by instituting reforms designed to limit civil rights and politicize the bureaucracy. Here, I examine the inclusion of women during this decade of democratic reduction and argue that the simultaneous increase in reserved seats for women was due in part to the benefits of associating with women in the context of declining democracy.

After the 2001 election, Bangladesh shifted away from its democratic potential in several ways. First, while the system still allowed competition between the two major parties, both spent significant parts of the subsequent decade boycotting the legislature (and therefore disempowering it).

Second, restrictions on the press increased during this time and, in 2003, the government began detaining journalists and editors who reported unfavorable news (Freedom House 2004). In addition, under the guise of "Operation Clean Heart"—an anti-crime initiative begun in 2002— the army arrested 11,000 people, including several major political figures (Freedom House 2004). Shortly thereafter, the government also arrested the president of one of Bangladesh's largest anti-poverty NGOs and, while the charge was embezzlement, this man had been a popular and well-known critic of the government.[8] Finally, the years 2001–2006 marked a time of unprecedented politicization of the bureaucracy. Osman (2010) explains that, during this period:

> the regime employed a laboratory to search for the loyal officials and also the disloyal. Explaining the process, a bureaucrat said, "People having green signal in the software were promoted while those with red signals indicating the disloyal were dropped." (P. 321)

The government was using the bureaucracy to advance its objectives; the goal was not to implement the law fairly and evenly, but rather to politicize the bureaucracy enough to ensure that policy outcomes benefitted the government. During this decade, therefore, it is clear that Bangladesh was a classic hybrid regime.

The status of women in Bangladesh is complicated, to say the least, and thus establishing the incongruency cost in this environment is also complicated. Two women have served as prime ministers, but both had significant familial legacies in politics. Further, Bangladesh is a very religious country—about 90% of its citizens identify as Muslim—and thus all women leaders in this country must navigate the difficult balance of being both pious in a very traditional, patriarchal religion (e.g., observing the Islamic dress code of covering their heads in public and attending patriarchal religious functions [Chowdhury 2009]), while also demonstrating that they can be effective politicians. Further, while the constitution explicitly declares women's rights to be equal to men, "legal discrimination against women exists through the religious laws relating to marriage, divorce, child custody, and property inheritance" (Halder 2004, p. 38). In addition, while women's literacy rate was only about 53% in 2008,[9] the government constructed a comprehensive bureaucracy to further the advancement of women in society and politics (Khan et al. 2005). Thus, it is a mistake to conceptualize Bangladesh as completely exclusionary of women's leadership but also an error to argue that the political culture is inclusionary to women.

The constitutional amendment which established a set of reserved seats in the legislature further illustrates the complicated nature of women's inclusion in the politics of Bangladesh. The first amendment to guarantee seats for women was passed in 1972—only one year after independence— and reserved 15 seats in the legislature for women. This amendment and all following amendments on reserved seats, however, carried a sunset clause, which meant that the reserved seat requirement would expire after 10 years. In subsequent years, the legislature usually voted to institute a new reserved seat law, but not always: in the 2001 election, for example, there was no quota for women (Paasilinna 2016). In May of 2004, a constitutional amendment passed that raised the percentage of reserved seats for women to 45 seats or about 13% of the legislature—its highest level ever.[10]

The adoption of this quota at this moment in time seems likely due to the elites' determination that the benefits of women's inclusion outweighed the costs, with perhaps the most obvious being the international responsiveness benefit. Following the logic of Bush (2011), the rational opportunist in this political context should have seen the possibility of financial gain through women's inclusion. After all, Bangladesh is a very poor country and does receive foreign aid, so it seems likely that international aid played a role in their decision to adopt the new quota. However, because of the relatively small amount of aid that the country receives, it is unlikely that this is the only causal driver. For example, the World Bank tracks the net official development assistance received as a percentage of Gross National Income (GNI): in 2001, Bangladesh's development assistance was 1.8% of GNI, which increased to 2.1% in 2008. Another measure of foreign aid, the net official development assistance per capita, was 7.8% in 2001 and increased to 13.9% in 2008.[11] These increases are not unimportant, but it is critical to note that foreign aid increased in general during the past 15 years and that many countries receive dramatically higher levels of development assistance. There is, however, little reason to believe that the reserved seat law was adopted due to a substantial domestic responsiveness benefit. Women's interest groups, while making some headway in normalizing women's presence in politics—see, for example, the Bangladesh Mahila Parishad (BMP) discussed in Panday (2008)—have had limited success on generating a societal push for women's inclusion.

In addition to the benefit found from international responsiveness, it seems safe to assume that the rational opportunist analyzing the threat cost of women's inclusion in the legislature would conclude that it is low in this particular institutional context. The legislature during this time was "ineffective and dysfunctional" due to the "deliberate bypassing by the ruling party and desertion by the opposition" (Moniruzzaman 2009, p. 124) and thus was an unlikely stepping stone for legislators to move up through the party ranks. Further, because women's inclusion in the legislature was facilitated through reserved seats, they could be marginalized and prevented from having access to the kind of power that would contribute to their future advancement in the party. As Chowdhury (2009) explains:

> the female Members of Parliament from the reserved seats were considered as mere "ornaments" due to the absence of any effective participation by them in parliament. This arrangement does not represent women's electorate and the female members do not have any influence in governmental policies and decisions. (P. 557)

Thus, the reserved seats allow a visible but benign—and, in fact, dependent— avenue of political participation for women while reestablishing the general tier of parliament as the domain of male politicians.

The adoption of a stronger gender quota in Bangladesh, therefore, can be reasonably viewed as a low cost and primarily symbolic gesture. The question is, however, was this gesture simply for the international audience?

Or is there reason to believe that there was a potential incongruity benefit from women's inclusion that could restore some of the recently lost legitimacy of this regime? I argue that there is indeed reason to believe that women's inclusion was in part driven by the elites' desire to replace lost domestic legitimacy. The year that the government voted to reinstate the reserved seat law was a particularly bad year for civil rights in this country. As Riaz (2005) explains, "the year 2004 was not typical for Bangladesh; unfortunately, it was worse than usual. The country's fragile democracy suffered serious reversals" (p. 112). Perhaps the epitome of these reversals can be found, interestingly, in the *same* constitutional amendment that reinstated the reserved seat law. The Fourteenth Amendment to the constitution established 45 reserved seats for women in the legislature, but it also included an unrelated provision: it extended the retirement age for judges from 65 to 67 years old. This may seem like an innocuous change but, to the people of Bangladesh, it was actually incredibly controversial. By extending the retirement age to 67, the government ensured that the "non-political caretaker government" (NCG) that assumes power during the election so as to ensure fairness would be led by a Chief Justice who was known to be a vocal advocate of the current government, not the opposition (Khan 2015). Thus, while one part of this amendment was clearly detrimental to democracy, the reinstatement of reserved seats for women could have been the government's way of signaling a renewed commitment to democracy. In other words, the timing of the quota reinstatement suggests that women's increased inclusion was a strategic effort to give the citizens the perception of democracy and inclusiveness, while simultaneously reducing the actual level of democracy in the country.

CONCLUSION

As of mid-2018, eight countries have either eclipsed gender parity in the lower house of their legislature or are within 5% of the 50% threshold: Rwanda, Cuba, Bolivia, Mexico, Grenada, Namibia, Nicaragua, and Costa Rica.[12] Of these eight countries, Freedom House classifies three as having the rights and freedoms of democracies (Grenada, Namibia, and Costa Rica) and the remaining five as non-democracies. Two of these five are essentially authoritarian (Rwanda and Cuba), while three are in the grey zone of the classic hybrid regimes: Bolivia, Mexico, and Nicaragua. This means that the majority of countries currently closest to gender parity in their legislatures are non-democracies, which suggests that the frequent assumption that women's presence facilitates democratic behavior may be misguided.

As I have argued in this chapter, it seems more likely that elites may be using women's presence as a signal of—and really a substitute for—democracy. Leaders in hybrid regimes have an incentive to "perform" democracy while simultaneously keeping actual democratic behaviors as tightly restricted as possible. Because of this, I argued that the incongruity benefit associated with women in these conditions is substantial, and is particularly high when the regime is removing rights or democratic processes. To test this theory, I offered an analysis of women's descriptive representation in 27 hybrid regimes over a period of 16 years, and found evidence that there is a significant relationship between a drop in democratic characteristics in a regime and an increase in the presence of women legislators. Then, I focused on two particular hybrid regimes, Ethiopia and Bangladesh, and offered conceptualizations of elite inclusion calculations under conditions of declining democratic traits in both countries. The evidence from these case studies suggests that it was not just a coincidence that elites in both countries adopted gender quotas while simultaneously lowering the level of democracy but instead a strategic move of performing democracy by manipulating women's legislative presence.

Conclusion, Implications, and Future Research

OVERVIEW

In the preceding chapters of this book, I analyzed scenarios in which, according to my central thesis, men in power had an incentive to facilitate women's increased presence in politics. I argued that a majority of men in politics are rational opportunists, not angels nor devils, and thus that there must be a self-interested reason why they are allowing and even supporting women—that is, additional competitors—in the political sphere. In chapter 2, I discussed the existing literature on elite strategy and women's representation and built a conceptual framework of the competing individual and partisan motivations that rational opportunists face when contemplating the addition of women to the political sphere under status quo conditions. I conceptualized these motivations as costs and benefits and argued that women's presence in the government rests in part on male elites' strategic calculation of the value of their inclusion. In addition, I considered the effect of changing political conditions on the results of the inclusion calculation and suggested that a break in the status quo causes the calculation of women's inclusion to become more obvious. Rather than the relatively static calculation found under normal conditions, the status quo break changes the values of multiple variables, which in turn triggers a more dramatic change in women's inclusion. In chapter 3, I engaged the common stereotypes associated with women, with a particular focus on the traits that fall into the "women are wonderful" categorization. I argued that, because of these assumed personality traits, women's presence sends a signal: women are not interpreted simply as neutral representatives of their district or party but instead trigger citizens to believe that the institutions they are associated with are more honest, inclusive, and democratic. This association, in turn, is a benefit of their inclusion, but only outweighs the costs of women's increased presence and power under certain conditions. Political elites can therefore strategically use women legislators to give citizens the impression of a new embrace of honesty or even democracy, even if those elites have no sincere interest in including women in the political process.

In chapters 4, 5, and 6, I presented evidence suggesting that elites, as rational opportunists, tend to increase women's inclusion when being associated with women's stereotypical traits becomes more valuable to the party or government. The evidence in these chapters is all circumstantial— there is no way to acquire direct evidence of elites strategically feminizing their governments or parties—and thus my goal was to present indirect evidence from multiple angles of inclusion. In chapter 4, I focused on the context of corruption scandal revelations and began with an analysis of candidate selection under these conditions in three cases: Spain, Portugal, and Ireland. Further, I offered an analysis of women's legislative descriptive representation, because one can make the case that if voters are more likely to elect women in this context then the elites are certain to take note of this behavior. Voter response to candidates, in other words, should drive elite strategies in democracies. In chapter 5, I analyzed a different method of inclusion—the adoption of a gender quota—and discussed the costs and benefits of quota adoption from the perspective of male elites. I argued that one of the reasons why quotas have exploded on the world scene is due to the benefit that they bring existing elites; in some respects, this method of inclusion can potentially be the most advantageous for maintaining the patriarchal power structure. In addition, I offered case studies of gender quota adoption in Italy and Argentina in the post-scandal context and suggested that their adoption was due to the benefits of women's inclusion to existing elites. In chapter 6, I focused on the context of declining democratic behaviors in hybrid regimes. Because of the more direct control over election results in hybrid regimes, I presented an analysis of women's legislative representation as an expression of the preferences of elites rather than voters and found that women's inclusion tends to increase as a country's democratic traits fade away. In addition, I offered case study analyses of Ethiopia and Bangladesh, two hybrid regimes that adopted gender quotas as they simultaneously removed civil rights and accountability mechanisms. In sum, all three of these chapters offered evidence of a correlation between changing conditions that increase the value of feminine stereotypes and women's inclusion; as legitimacy declined, I argued, women's presence became a valuable symbol of good governance and democratic behavior, thus creating an incentive for parties and governments to strategically feminize.

IMPLICATIONS

The implications of my findings are extensive and important for both scholars and women aspirants to consider. Arguably the most important implication for gender and politics scholars is that our field should no longer overlook the role of men as gatekeepers in our analyses of women's descriptive representation. That is, the evidence presented in this book suggests that male elites make strategic decisions about women's representation based on its value to those male elites' electoral futures. This means, therefore, that when we look only at the institutional, structural, and cultural factors that impact women's representation, we are missing an important piece of the puzzle. We must also consider how existing elites—the vast majority of whom are men—conceptualize the costs and benefits of increasing women's presence and power, and how their conceptualization affects women's descriptive representation.

In additions, these results suggest that scholars, as well as international organizations and state departments, may need to stop using women's descriptive representation as a measurement of equality and/

or democracy. There are several examples of this in academic scholar-ship alone, and it is particularly prevalent in the recent trend of creating new democracy indices. For example, the Democracy Barometer is an index that purports to measure the quality of democracy across regimes. This index is built using a wealth of variables to quantify the level of freedom, control, and equality, in a country and also includes a measure of women's legislative representation in an effort to capture whether the regime is representative of "all citizens' preferences."[1] Another example of this trend in scholarly research is the recent contribution of Coppedge et al. (2011). Their article suggests that we need a new approach to the conceptualization and measurement of democracy, and they offer sev-eral possible indicators of democracy that could be built into an index and compared across regimes. One of the categories of indicators is "gender equality," and it consists of variables that measure "the extent to which women achieve equal representation in the legislature" (p. 256). With this claim they assume, just as the Democracy Barometer does, that women's legislative representation is strongly correlated with democracy. In other words, both indices have fallen into the if/then trap outlined in chapter 3, in which they assume that the mere presence of women in a legislature means that a state is more democratic than one with fewer women, all else being equal. While this association is understandable, this book offers substantial evidence that it may be misguided. That is, because there is a strategic benefit to be gained from associating with women in certain contexts, we cannot interpret women's presence in pol-itics as a reflection of their equality or as an accurate measure of how well the democracy is functioning. Rather, as is the case in several countries with record-breaking levels of women's representation, women's power remains low and limited and the regime remains thoroughly authori-tarian. For example, one of the most consistent findings in the substan-tive representation literature is that while women in the legislature can influence some facets of legislative politics, their presence is unlikely to result in the passage of even basic women's rights policies (Franceschet and Piscopo 2008; Franceschet 2010; Htun et al. 2013). We cannot as-sume, therefore, that women legislators have access to real power or independent decision-making authority, and thus they should not be used as a measure of equality or democracy.

Further, scholars should pause before utilizing descriptive representation as a measure of good governance, because it perpetuates the idea that women are like-minded symbols. That is, while the association of women with economic modernization was initially done, at least in part, to facilitate women's equality, one could argue that it inadvertently perpetuates inequality by reducing women to a single-minded group. Thus, while the "country gender assessment" that bases aid decisions on descriptive representation will drive up the number of women in power, it simultaneously undermines cultural advancement away from objectifying women. To break from our status as objects, women must be viewed as complicated, different from one another, and, in short, human; our continued association with stereotypical traits only serves to reinforce those stereotypes.

This book also offers several implications for women seeking to increase their presence and power in government, though unfortunately these implications are troubling. At the foundation of this book is the assumption that all people continue to live in patriarchies, and thus the decisions of male elites have a powerful effect on women's ascension. This means, in turn, that one should not build a strategy for gaining power that minimizes or ignores the reality of the patriarchy, even though that reality can be disturbing and difficult to face. Thus, with this new perspective on the power of men in determining women's representation, it seems that the path of least resistance to women's power should include a strategy that somehow benefits existing (male) elites. For example, my results suggest that women who are seeking power may find a potential winning strategy in emphasizing their stereotypical feminine traits, assuming that the political context is appropriate. This is not without cost—the more women who claim that they are "naturally" more honest than men, the more this stereotype will stick in the human psyche and reinforce a false difference—but the reality is that it is an effective strategy. Thus, women who are considering a run for office should consider the context and, assuming that the context generates an increased value for traits associated with women, then consciously market themselves to gatekeepers and voters as an asset because of the usefulness of their feminine stereotypes for feminizing the party or government.

Building from this, it also follows that women seeking power must be mindful to not alienate or distance themselves too much from male elites, even in contexts in which the cultural tide is recognizing the, at times, deeply problematic behavior of men (e.g., #metoo). That is, because men are a fundamental element of women's ascent to power, the strategy of ignoring or bypassing them will rarely be effective. Instead, women need to cultivate allies among those male elites who, according to their inclusion calculations, have the least to lose and the most to gain from women's increased presence and power. For example, the foundational logic of the threat cost is that distance matters: men at similar ranks of power will feel more threatened by women's presence at higher levels of power than men who have significantly higher levels of power than those women. This suggests, in turn, that it is a beneficial strategy for women seeking to increase their power to align themselves with the highest-ranking male, not with the male in close vicinity; for example, send your request for a promotion to the president of the company or the leader of the party, not to your co-manager or that local-level elite you've known for years. That being said, the threat cost is only one variable in the inclusion calculation, so this is not a guaranteed path for success, but it is one way that women can lower the cost of their own inclusion.

If one accepts the evidence that suggests that men are rational opportunists rather than angels or devils, then unfortunately this means that women should not assume that men—even allied men—are willing to dismantle the patriarchy. That is, we are in a time in many cultures in which it is savvy for men to state a commitment to diversity, or to declare that women deserve equality; these claims are not necessarily false but— understanding the incentive structure of the rational opportunist—these claims do not signal a willingness of men to actually sacrifice their power. In other words, one need not assume that men who claim to be allies are lying—some of them sincerely believe their words and the value of women's equality in general—but one should be cautious about expecting those men to actually step aside and facilitate women's ascent at the expense of their own power; this is not an if/then relationship in which *if* a man expresses support for feminism *then* he'll be willing to give up his power. The environment may appear to be equalized because of the growing cultural norm of positively framing women's advancement, but supportive declarations of "girl power!" or wearing pussy hats should not be viewed as akin to a willingness to step aside. Thus, even with men who are allies, there is a tipping point of women's power at which the loss to men's own power will be too much to bear—that is, the cost is too high— and they will withdraw their support; this is not because they are devils, but rather because they are rational actors who fundamentally want to protect their privileged status.

An additional implication of this research is that, because women's political inclusion is at least in part dependent on the decisions of certain men, women who are ascending should anticipate backlash from the men who stand to lose power and privilege because of their ascension. Faludi's (1991) conceptualization of backlash is as more of a unified, societal response to women's attempted advances in equality; she refers to it as a "recurring phenomenon," explaining that "it returns every time women begin to make some headway toward equality, a seemingly inevitable early frost to the culture's brief flowering of feminism" (p. 46). My conceptualization of backlash is different—I envision a more individualized response, one grounded in a conceptualization of power as a zero-sum game. It is not a general societal reaction and is not driven by devilish men who delight in oppression. Rather, backlash in the perspective of the inclusion calculation occurs on the individual level, as the negative reaction of a single man whose own inclusion calculation is different from that of the men who determined that women's presence was more of a benefit than a cost.[2] In short, just because one rational opportunist decides that women's inclusion will be beneficial enough to merit the associated costs, this does not mean that all other men in the environment will agree with or accept the decision; even those men in the same government or political party may calculate the value of women's inclusion differently. There is little that can be done to mitigate this backlash—it is, after all, a rational response to the loss of power—but it is valuable to emphasize that the backlash these included women might feel has nothing to do with them as individuals.

They should not take this personally, but rather remember that because we continue to live in patriarchies, women in power will face resistance from men who are losing power. No amount of hard work or perfection will lessen it, though a tough shell will be helpful to surviving it.[3]

Arguably, the most important implication of the research in this book is that we should be more hesitant about advising women that our status in society and politics can change if we "lean in" or "be more ambitious." Let me be clear: I am not discouraging women's ambition. Rather, similar to Piscopo (2019), I am suggesting that we need to be more nuanced about telling women that our lack of power in society is due to our own lack of ambition or confidence. For example, Lawless and Fox (2005, 2010) and McElroy and Marsh (2010) argue that the continuing under-representation of women in politics is due in part to the ambition gap—that is, women do not want to run and/or women do not have the confidence to run for office. The punchline of this research is that women need to step up in order to change our position in society; it is on us, in other words, to change our fate. This is a valuable suggestion—it is a good thing to encourage women's agency—but it overstates the neutrality of the political realm. That is, women may lean in, they may run for office, but the individual gatekeepers are male. And, assuming these gatekeepers are rational actors, they have an incentive to exclude future competitors and perpetuate the patriarchal system that benefits them. The gatekeepers are, in short, rational opportunists, and these opportunists are more likely to facilitate women's representation when it somehow benefits them, not necessarily just because women are "leaning in." Therefore, it is important to both encourage women's ambition *and* recognize the continuing role of men in their success; as disturbing as it might seem, the reality of the patriarchy means that women's advancement cannot be achieved without the consent of men.

FUTURE RESEARCH

In many ways, this book is only the first step in understanding the role of male gatekeepers in women's representation, and thus many possible paths for future research are available to scholars. For example, throughout this book, I worked from the assumption that women are associated with communal personality traits. I argued that these stereotypical traits are relatively consistent across countries and time, and that what changes is their value; that is, in some conditions, associating with these traits is an asset, in others it is not. But what about those conditions when citizens see women who actively violate the expectations for gendered behavior by being caught in, for example, a massive corruption scandal? How does this change the incongruity benefit, and how long does that change last? In 2011, the Inter-Parliamentary Union (IPU) noted a significant drop in women's representation in Peru largely due to the "the Canchaya effect," in which the suspected corruption of Congresswomen Elsa Canchaya started a snowball effect of corruption scandals breaking across the government, some of which involved women. The IPU report states that the "the honesty of women in leadership was questioned when similar cases of corruption involving Congresswomen arose" and that this led to the big decrease in both their selection as candidates on party lists and their legislative presence (IPU Report 2011, p. 3). Thus, in this context, the incongruity benefit seemed to be deactivated; citizens had recent examples of women acting counter to their gendered expectations and thus, even in this context of political scandals breaking, this benefit did not materialize. This illustrates, therefore, the complicated reality of gender stereotypes and thus suggests that more research is necessary—research that allows for variation in citizens associating women with these feminine traits.

Another path for future researchers is to introduce variation in the general personalities of women and add that variable to the inclusion calculation. That is, my analysis assumed that all women are the same in the eyes of elites, but this is not necessarily true. I noted this briefly in chapter 1 when I discussed the qualifications of women in the political sphere; I explained that, while we should not assume that women candidates are less qualified than men, there may be an incentive for male elites who see a benefit in women's inclusion to choose women who are most likely to maintain the patriarchy. In other words, a rational opportunist lowers the threat cost of women's inclusion by selecting women who generally seem to accept the patriarchy (perhaps by a display of support for traditional gender roles) and/or have limited ambition. Krook (2009) notes this phenomenon in her analysis of the adoption of a gender quota in Argentina, finding that:

> many of the women being placed on lists were closely tied to their party leadership, often through a personal connection, meaning that women associated with feminist issues were rarely selected as candidates. (P. 171)

On the other hand, if citizens view those women as supporting the existing power structure too much, then they may not bring the same level of incongruity benefit to the party or government that the more "disruptive" women would bring. Adding a "fight the power" woman to the candidate list may send a different signal to citizens than adding a loyal widow who frequently discusses her husband's legacy; that is, the feminist female candidate may be worth the additional threat cost if she also delivers additional incongruity benefit. Or perhaps this difference among women only matters in certain systems—such as those with a personal vote—or when they are placed at certain list positions. In any case, it is possible that the differences in approaches/personalities of women trigger different costs and benefits associated with their inclusion, and this should be further examined.

This book presented two possible contexts in which the stereotypical traits associated with women increase in value—hybrid regimes and postcorruption scandal elections—but future research could examine other circumstances in which being associated with people who are assumed to be honest, inclusive, and just naturally democratic could come in handy. The proactive use of feminine stereotypes could also be a beneficial strategy in, for example, highly divided societies with a recent, peacefully concluded civil conflict. In this scenario, the strong divisions in society generate an incentive for the government to appear inclusive and cooperative and, because of the recent peaceful conclusion to conflict, citizens are less likely to be looking for an aggressive defense of the interests of their group alone (i.e., stereotypical male and leadership traits have lost value).

Instead, it is temporarily advantageous to be associated with traditionally feminine traits, and thus male elites are likely to strategically increase the presence of women in the legislature.

Another avenue for future research concerns intersectionality. Throughout this book, I have employed the assumption that women—no matter their other racial, ethnic, religious, or sexual identities—are associated with a particular set of traditional feminine stereotypes. While this is generally true, it is admittedly an over-simplification; women of a certain ethnic identity, for example, may be associated with different personality traits than women in the same country but of a different ethnicity. The same trend can be applied to sexuality: women who identify as lesbian may be associated with different stereotypical personality traits than those who are publicly heterosexual. The addition of intersectionality to this sort of analysis will be challenging because, for example, there are very few women in politics who do *not* identify with the dominant ethnic, racial, or religious groups in their country and even fewer who are publicly lesbian. Further, because the stereotypes associated with ethnic, racial, and other under-represented groups tend to vary by country, research that engages the intersectionality lens will probably need to be performed as country-by-country, or with a small-N, analysis. These challenges, however, do not negate the necessity of this line of research.

The final avenue of potential future research concerns scenarios in which, rather than decreasing, the incongruity cost increases dramatically. That is, this book focused on contexts in which women's stereotypes become assets rather than detriments—scenarios in which the typical incongruity cost transitions to a potential benefit. But it seems feasible that, just as there are contexts when the cost lessens, there could also be scenarios in which the incongruity cost increases dramatically, thereby making the inclusion of women unacceptable. Two scenarios come to mind in which strategic feminization would do more harm than good to the government, even under conditions of declining legitimacy. First, when a government is engaged in active elite-driven conflict, as was the case in the Central African Republic (CAR). Second, when a leader or government cultivates legitimacy through hyper-masculinity, as is the case in Russia.

The CAR suffered a dramatic loss in its degree of democratization during the twenty-first century; both the Freedom House and Polity2 measures of democratization demonstrate a strong downward trajectory during the past two decades. However, although it could have been beneficial to this regime to adopt a gender quota as a method to, according to my argument, signal a commitment to honesty and democracy even as they remove civil rights, no gender quota was adopted by either the government or any of the political parties. This exception, therefore, presents a valuable opportunity to consider a scenario in which strategic feminization would have been a poor strategy: continuous elite-driven conflict. Simultaneous to the decline in democracy, a steady level of severe civil conflict occurred in the CAR: the Major Episodes of Political Violence data set, which tracks episodes of violence that include at least 500 directly related deaths, categorized the CAR as at level 3 of civil warfare from 2005 to 2015, which denotes "serious political violence."[4] In fact, because of the level of violence perpetrated by the state against its own citizens, including torture and arbitrary arrest and detention, as well as the violence between the state and non-state actors (such as rebel militias), Gerlach (2010) classifies the CAR as an "extremely violent society." It is particularly important to emphasize that ethnicity and religion have *not* been the basis of this continuous conflict; rather, as Isaacs-Martin (2016) explains: "Since 2002 much of the conflicts and violence has been popularly attributed to competing political elites rather than to strife between communities of different ethnic identities" (p. 30). If the conflict was rooted in ethnic or religious cleavages, then adopting a gender quota could be a beneficial strategy. In that scenario, the government could strategically use women's presence or even a purely symbolic quota to send a signal of inclusion, without having to actually include any additional ethnic or religious groups in governance. However, because the basis of this conflict is competing elites, most of whom are interested in controlling the substantial reserve of natural resources in the CAR, sending a signal of inclusion is not an appropriate strategy. Instead, the better strategy is to maintain an aggressive posture and signal traditionally masculine traits so as to never give the appearance of any sort of weakness or willingness to compromise. In this environment, therefore, the adoption of a gender quota and the resulting association with women would have been a dangerous maneuver for the government.

Another country in which strategic feminization is never a good strategy is modern-day Russia. President Putin has spent the past two decades chipping away at the democratic elements in Russian institutions, centralizing power in his hands while decreasing the presence of even minimal checks on his government. However, while this steady decline in democratic behavior should, according to my theory, create an incentive to adopt a quota or increase the descriptive representation of women due to the potential legitimacy boost, there are no legislated or voluntary party gender quotas in Russia and women's representation remains low. There are a multitude of possible reasons for this, including the fact that post-communist regimes are particularly unfriendly to gender quotas due to their association with communism (Ferber and Raabe 2003; Cook and Nechemias 2009), as well as because of the weak presence of women's movements in Russia (Salmenniemi and Adamson 2015). But in addition, if it is the case that the inclusion of women feminizes the government, then any gender quota would undermine the hyper-masculinity foundational to Putin's legitimacy and would thus be an unacceptable choice. This is not simply a story of Russia being particularly patriarchal—one of the core assumptions of this book is that all regimes are patriarchal—but rather the fact that the Kremlin *systematically* emphasizes Putin's hyper-masculine behaviors and heterosexuality in an effort to cultivate legitimacy. Sperling (2015) offers countless examples of the Kremlin's strategy to depict Putin as the epitome of masculinity, arguing that:

Fostering a macho image has been one of the central features of Russian president Vladimir Putin's political legitimation strategy. Following his first election to the presidency in March 2000, Putin's numerous masculinity-displaying feats have included his "saving" a crew of journalists from a Siberian tiger, zooming around a track in a Formula-One racecar, braving rough seas to garner a skin sample collected with a crossbow from a gray whale, and showing off his martial arts skills. (P. 29)

Thus, in a political context in which the government is systematically reinforcing its own hyper-masculinity in an effort to cultivate legitimacy, the inclusion of women would, according to my theory, be a foolish decision. The Kremlin has built Putin's legitimacy on hyper-masculine notions of strength and aggression—arguably more than any other regime that exists in the world today—and the inclusion of women would undermine that strategy by feminizing the government. Russia under Putin's reign, therefore, will never adopt a gender quota or boost the presence of women in the legislature, not because the country is unusually patriarchal or misogynist, but because it would undermine their current method of cultivating legitimacy.

YOUR MOMENT OF ZEN

To end on a positive note, while women's political advancement may be limited by their strategic usefulness to men in power, that does not change the fact that they are slowly increasing their presence in governing institutions. That is, their "usefulness" in certain contexts has helped increase their access to power, and thus they can capitalize on the fact that, while they don't control the room, they are at least now allowed inside of it. Even 30 years ago, women did not have the kind of access and influence that they now have today, and this achievement should be celebrated. That being said, the continued advancement of women may depend, at least in part, on an awareness of the continuing power of the patriarchy. Women should not pretend that they are conceived of as equals or that the playing field is level; this misconception leads to the false premise that their success is entirely up to them, and thus that working harder is the solution to their oppression. Rather, by staying aware that they are not viewed as equals and that their inclusion depends—at least in part—on their usefulness to male elites, they can build strategies for inclusion that consciously engage this reality. Women should, in other words, always remember that their exclusion from government is not simply a product of their own lack of effort or ability, but rather a rational response of those in power to keep their power.

Lists of Positive and Negative Traits Presented to Participants

POSITIVE TRAITS OFFERED TO PARTICIPANTS:

Aggressive	Forgiving	Modest
Ambitious	Friendly	Outspoken
Appreciative	Gentle	Patient
Attractive	Helpful	Pacifying or Peace-making
Cautious	Honest	Rational
Cheerful	Imaginative	Sensitive
Confident	Intelligent	Sincere
Considerate	Independent	Strong
Courageous	Kind	Tactful
Energetic	Logical	Tolerant

NEGATIVE TRAITS OFFERED TO PARTICIPANTS:

Absent-minded	Dreamy	Meek
Anxious	Egotistical	Moody
Arrogant	Fearful	Nervous
Awkward	Forceful	Opportunistic
Bossy	Frivolous	Reckless

Careless	Fussy	Rude
Cold	Greedy	Shy
Conceited	High-strung	Stubborn
Cowardly	Hostile	Submissive
Cynical	Inhibited	Timid
Dependent	Intolerant	Weak
Dishonest	Loud	Whiny

Descriptions and Sources of All Variables used
in Chapter 6 Regression

Change in Level of Democracy (Polity2)= Composite, ordinal measure of the level of democracy/autocracy of a state based on such indicators as the regulation and competitiveness of voter participation and the constraints on the chief executive. Scale ranges from –10, applied to states considered to have maximum levels of authoritarian traits (e.g., North Korea), to +10 for states with maximum levels of democratic traits (e.g., Australia).

Source: http://www.systemicpeace.org/polityproject.html

Gender Quota Law= Dichotomous variable

Source: https://www.idea.int/data-tools/data/gender-quotas

Proportional Representation= Dichotomous variable

Source: http://www.idea.int/data-tools/question-view/130357

http://www.ipu.org/parline-e/mod-electoral.asp

Women's Literacy= Continuous variable: Percentage of women in country who are literate.

Source: http://www.uis.unesco.org/Education/Documents/literacy-statistics-trends-1985-2015.pdf

Civil Conflict= Composite, ordinal variable tracking the presence and level of civil violence and/or warfare during the election year.

Source: Major Episodes of Political Violence and Conflict Regions, 1946–2015. Created by the Center for Systemic Peace. www.systemicpeace.org

Conclusion of Civil Conflict= Dichotomous variable that captures whether civil conflict concluded during the years preceding the election.

Source: Major Episodes of Political Violence and Conflict Regions, 1946–2015. Created by the Center for Systemic Peace. www.systemicpeace.org

Foreign Aid Received= Continuous variable: the net official development assistance (ODA) received as a percentage of gross national income (calculated by World Bank).

Source: http://data.worldbank.org/indicator/DT.ODA.ODAT.GN.ZS?locations=ZM

Percentage of Practicing Muslims= Continuous variable: percentage of people who identify as Muslim.

Source: http://www.thearda.com/Archive/Files/Descriptions/WRPGLOBL.asp

Years Since Women's Suffrage=Continuous variable: number of years between women's suffrage being granted and the legislative election.

Source: http://womensuffrage.org/?page_id=69

GDP per Capita= Continuous variable

Source: http://data.worldbank.org/indicator/NY.GDP.PCAP.CD

CHAPTER 1

1. Ditchburn, Jennifer. 2015. "'Because it's 2015': Trudeau Forms Canada's 1st Gender-Balanced Cabinet." *CBCnews*, November 4. http://www.cbc.ca/news/politics/canada-trudeau-liberal-government-cabinet-1.3304590 (October 15, 2018).

2. *The Telegraph*. 2012. "French Female Minister Wolf-Whistled in Parliament." July 20. http://www.telegraph.co.uk/news/worldnews/europe/france/9414590/French-female-minister-wolf-whistled-in-parliament.html (October 15, 2018).

3. Mitchell, Austin. 2014. "Ed's 'Apparet-Chicks' Are Exactly What My Party Doesn't Need: As Miliband Crams Labour with Women, Veteran MP Austin Mitchell Shares His Hilarious (and Highly Personal) View." *Daily Mail*, August16. http://www.dailymail.co.uk/debate/article-2726957/Eds-apparat-chicks-exactly-party-DOESNT-need-As-Miliband-crams-Labour-women-veteran-MP-Austin-Mitchell-shares-hilarious-highly-personal-view.html (October 15, 2018).

4. Though let's make a note to perhaps look into that option in the future.

CHAPTER 2

1. In chapter 5, I reconsider the variables in the inclusion calculation using a different method of inclusion: the adoption of a gender quota.

2. It is important to note that as the number of women incumbents rises, this particular effect will decrease in power. This argument is based on the assumption that there are more male incumbents than women incumbents and thus that displacing an incumbent usually means displacing a man.

3. "CEDAW" refers to the Convention on the Elimination of All Forms of Discrimination against Women, and was adopted by the United Nations General Assembly in 1979.

CHAPTER 3

1. https://www.ndi.org/gender-women-democracy (October 1, 2016).

2. These sculpted women are mostly naked and have their eyes closed, but that discussion is probably best saved for another book.

3. Blume, Mary. 2004. "The French Icon Marianne à la Mode." *New York Times*, July 16.

4. Buckley, Chris. 2014. "The Rise and Fall of the Goddess of Democracy." *New York Times*, June 1.

5. https://www.ndi.org/gender-women-democracy.(October 1, 2016).

6. These universities offered very diverse student profiles: one is a large, public, urban university, another is a small, public, rural university, and the third is a small, private, liberal arts college. The university in Canada is a large, public university. At all universities, I received approval to perform my experiment from the Human Subjects Review Boards. Leupold and Stevens was selected due to the high proportion of their workers who strongly support right-wing candidates and causes; by including them, I increased the ideological variation of my survey pool.

7. Research by Druckman and Kam (2011), however, demonstrates that using students as experimental participants does not, as has long been claimed, automatically generate external validity problems.

8. This survey was performed from 2010 to 2013, and thus before Hillary Clinton announced her bid for the presidency of the United States.

9. See Appendix I for the full list of positive and negative traits presented to participants.

10. There is little empirical evidence that supports the idea that citizens are correct in associating gender quotas/women in government with less corruption—that is, we have little proof that this "honest woman" stereotype is correct. While certain scholars, such as Swamy et al. (2001), present evidence that this stereotype is true, there is much debate as to the validity of those findings. As Goetz (2007) so eloquently explains, it is not that women are innately less corrupt but rather that they are regularly excluded from the circles of power and thus do not yet have the opportunity to be corrupt.

CHAPTER 4

1. None of the candidate lists explicitly stated the gender of each candidate, and therefore I coded the gender of the candidates based on each candidate's first and middle names. My coding methodology was as follows. I began by collecting common male and female names in each country from websites devoted to baby names (www.babynology.com, www.thinkbabynames.com, and www.babynamenetwork.com) and then coded the names on the party lists based on this collection. If the name was common and, according to the baby name websites, highly correlated with a particular gender (i.e., Thomas is almost always male, Betty is almost always female), then no further investigation was done—the name was coded based on the recommendation of the baby name websites. However, if the name was either uncommon or androgynous (i.e., Pat could be either male or female), then I searched for a picture of the candidate in question. If no picture was found, the candidate was removed from the analysis. In addition, if one website disagreed with another regarding whether a name was male or female, the name was considered androgynous and picture evidence was collected.

2. *AFX News*. 1994. "Spain's Garzon Resigned Due to Gonzalez's 'Passive Attitude' to Corruption." May 9.

3. Orin, Dominique. 1996. "Socialists' Good Record Marred by Corruption Scandals." *Agence France Presse*, February 29.

4. My decision to only include the biggest parties is driven by two factors. First, Spain has a tremendous number of parties and candidates running for office. For example, in the district of Barcelona, there were 22 parties running for election to the lower house in 2000. In addition, the average list size of each of these parties is 31 candidates. Thus, in this single district, there are about 682 candidates running for election. The arduous cost of coding all of those would be worthwhile if driven by a theoretical necessity, but that does not seem to be the case. Second, and arguably more important, the inclusion of only major parties in the analysis ensures that one of my foundational assumptions—political parties want to win—is accurate. Some of the small political parties in these systems are running to draw attention to a particular policy issue or to protest state action and thus may exhibit different nomination behaviors.

5. Things changed a bit in 1997 when both PSOE and IU created stronger and more effective voluntary quotas (Threlfall 2005; Verge 2010).

6. Roberts, Alison. 2014. "Portugal Plagued by Corruption Claims as ex-PM Socrates Held." *BBC News*, November 29.

7. *The Economist*. 2014. "Portugal's Visa Scandal: Buying Their Way In." November 22. http://www.economist.com/node/21633854/print (October 15, 2018).

8. It is unfortunately beyond the scope of this book to analyze the inclusion calculation at the district level, but this would be a fantastic next step—particularly for an eager graduate student looking for a challenging yet fascinating dissertation topic.

9. Clarity, James F. 1998. "A New Scandal Rocks Ireland, Provoking Turmoil in Parliament." *The New York Times*, December 17; Mullin, John. 1998. "Irish Politician in Corruption Investigation Found Dead." *The Guardian*, March 16.

10. Brophy, Karl. 2000. "Dáil in Crisis over Donations Claims." *The Mirror*, January 26; Downing, John, and Katie Hannon. 2000. "Lawlor Resigns as Corruption Threatens Others." *Irish Examiner*, July 8.

11. Mullin, John. 2000. "Corruption in the Eire." *The Guardian*, May 3; Sommerlad, Nick. 2002. "Shamed Bobby's Got to Go." *The Mirror*, April 10; *The Irish Times*. 2002. "Survival Instinct Saved Coalition Despite Scandals." April 25.

12. It is important to note that parties in Ireland do not present ordered lists of candidates (unlike Spain and Portugal). However, I refer to the slates of candidates presented by each party as "lists" to ease discussion.

13. Some measures of corruption, such as the Transparency International Corruption Perception Index, are good for a general sense of corruption, but not as valuable for both inter- and intra-country comparison due to the very low variance and large confidence intervals of the scores. Others, such as the measure created by Golden and Picci (2005), reflect the inner workings of government, but do not capture the ebb and flow or severity of corruption accusations.

14. It is important to note that I was careful to not simply code the number of times that a particular incident was mentioned by the newspapers. Once an incident was found, I created a detailed record of its existence such that I did not code multiple discussions of the same incident as multiple incidents.

15. This threshold is, admittedly, arbitrary. However, performing a case-by-case evaluation of each country introduces concerns of my own subjectivity, which (to me) is a greater sin. By creating a tipping point with clear and strict conditions, I am able to maintain a more objective approach to coding the independent variable.

16. It may be a bit surprising that such standard variables such as District Magnitude and GDP did not achieve significance in a model on women's representation, but the key is to note the coding of the dependent variable—it is not aggregate percentage of women in the legislature but rather a measurement of the relative change in the percentage of women since the previous election.

17. This variable is ordinal, coded from the survey question: "In general, how much effort do politicians and parties in this country make to induce voters with preferential benefits to cast their votes for them." The responses vary from (1) a negligible effort/none at all to (4) a major effort.

CHAPTER 5

1. See the Gender Quota Database for specifics: https://www.idea.int/data-tools/data/gender-quotas.

2. This description should elicit a mental image of Animal from *The Muppet Show*.

3. The legislators were: Paola Manzini, Giovanna Melandri, and Elena Montecchi. All three were members of the main social democrat party at the time: Democratici di Sinistra (DS). Montecchi was first elected to the legislature in 1986, while Manzini and Melandri first won their legislative seats in 1994. All interviews were recorded and are available from the author.

4. Mead, Gary. 1990. "From a Small Seed Authoritarianism Grows." *Financial Times*, May 8.

5. Barham, John. 1991. "Menem's Clean Image Burns as Argentina Fiddles." *Financial Times*, April 3.

6. Christian, Shirley. 1990. "Argentine Union Leader Blunt about Payoffs." *New York Times*, November 25.

7. Granovsky, Martin, and Colin Harding. 1991. "Menem Moves to Restore His Image; A Bribery Case Has Confirmed the Public's Cynical View of Political Morality." *The Independent*, January 19.

8. All quotations from the chamber debate on the quota bill are from the publicly released transcripts: "Republica Argentina: Diario de Sesiones. Cámara de Diputados de la Nacion: Sesion Ordinaria de Prorroga (Especial), Noviembre 6 y 7 de 1991." Translations are by the author and were reviewed by Bean Valdini and Jennifer Martinez.

CHAPTER 6

1. Marshall, Monty G., Ted Robert Gurr, and Keith Jaggers. 2017. "Polity IV Project: Political Regime Characteristics and Transitions, 1800–2016." *Center for Systemic Peace*. http://www.systemicpeace.org/inscrdata.html.

2. See Appendix II for detailed descriptions and sources of all variables.

3. Another way to model this would be PCSE with a lagged dependent variable. However, just as Achen (2000) explains, the lagged dependent variable biases the

coefficients and artificially inflates its own effect, and thus I do not use that model specification. However, it is important to note that even when I run this with a lagged dependent variable, the only variable that remains significant is my key explanatory variable, Polity2.

4. I am certain that differences across countries have an influence on my dependent variable, and thus the random effects model (rather than fixed effects) seems like the right choice. I performed a Hausman Test to be sure, and indeed the random effects model is the better choice.

5. Remember that this is a *relative* percentage change, not an aggregate change. For example, when I say that the relative percentage decreases by 34%, this does not mean that the percentage of women in the lower house went from, for example, 40% to 6%. Instead, because I'm referring to the relative change, this means, for example, a legislature with 40% would drop to about 26% women in the legislature (because a 34% decrease in a legislature of 40% women leaves about 26% women in the legislature).

6. *Africa News Service*. 2004. "Ethiopia: Ruling Party Wants More Women in Parliament." October 29.

7. Data source: http://www.ipu.org/wmn-e/classif.htm.May 5, 2017.

8. Waldman, Amy. 2004. "Bangladesh Arrests Director of Major Anti-Poverty Organization." *New York Times*, May 25.

9. http://www.uis.unesco.org/Education/Documents/literacy-statistics-trends-1985-2015.pdf.

10. https://www.idea.int/data-tools/data/gender-quotas/country-view/59/35.

11. http://data.worldbank.org/indicator/DT.ODA.ODAT.GN.ZS?locations=ZM; http://data.worldbank.org/indicator/DT.ODA.ODAT.PC.ZS.

12. Data from IPU: Women in National Parliaments (http://archive.ipu.org/wmn-e/classif.htm).

CHAPTER 7

1. http://www.democracybarometer.org/concept_en.html. Full citation of data set: Merkel, Wolfgang and Bochsler, Daniel (project leaders); Bousbah, Karima; Bühlmann, Marc; Giebler, Heiko; Hänni, Miriam; Heyne, Lea; Müller, Lisa; Ruth, Saskia; Wessels, Bernhard. (2016). Democracy Barometer. Codebook. Version 5. Aarau: Zentrum für Demokratie.

2. That being said, if a critical mass of men share this belief, then Faludi's conceptualization of a more societal wave of backlash is accurate as well. There is room for both understandings of backlash.

3. Remember, though, the angel and devil loopholes. There are small groups of men who will willingly sacrifice their own power so as to increase that of women (angels), just as there are small groups of men who will delight in blocking women's increased presence, even if it is not in their interest to do so (devils). But these men are likely the exception, not the rule.

4. Data set: Major Episodes of Political Violence and Conflict Regions, 1946–2015. Created by the Center for Systemic Peace. www.systemicpeace.org.

WORKS CITED

Aalen, Lovise, and Kjetil Tronvoll. 2009. "The End of Democracy? Curtailing Political and Civil Rights in Ethiopia." *Review of African Political Economy* 36.120: 193–207.

Abbink, Jon. 2006. "Discomfiture of Democracy? The 2005 Election Crisis in Ethiopia and Its Aftermath." *African Affairs* 105.419: 173–199.

Achen, Christopher H. 2000. "Why Lagged Dependent Variables Can Suppress the Explanatory Power of Other Independent Variables." Paper Presented at the Annual Meeting of the Political Methodology Section of the American Political Science Association, Los Angeles, July 20–22.

Alesina, Alberto, and David Dollar. 2000. "Who Gives Foreign Aid to Whom and Why?" *Journal of Economic Growth* 5.1: 33–63.

Alexander, Deborah, and Kristi Andersen. 1993. "Gender as a Factor in the Attribution of Leadership Traits." *Political Research Quarterly* 46.3: 527–545.

Ansolabehere, Stephen, James M. Snyder Jr., and Charles Stewart III. 2000. "Old Voters, New Voters, and the Personal Vote: Using Redistricting to Measure the Incumbency Advantage." *American Journal of Political Science* 44.1: 17–34.

Ashworth, Scott, and Ethan Bueno de Mesquita. 2008. "Electoral Selection, Strategic Challenger Entry, and the Incumbency Advantage." *The Journal of Politics* 70.4: 1006–1025.

Bach, Jean-Nicolas. 2011. "Abyotawi Democracy: Niether Revolutionary nor Democracti, a critica review f EPRDF's Conceptionoof Revolutionary Democracy in post-1991 Ethiopia." *Journal of Eastern African Studies* 5.4: 641–663.

Balán, Manuel. 2011. "Competition by Denunciation: The Political Dynamics of Corruption Scandals in Argentina and Chile." *Comparative Politics* 43.4: 459–478.

Baldez, Lisa. 2002. *Why Women Protest: Women's Movements in Chile.* New York: Cambridge University Press.

Baldez, Lisa. 2004. "Elected Bodies: The Gender Quota Law for Legislative Candidates in Mexico." *Legislative Studies Quarterly* 29.2: 231–258.

Baldez, Lisa. 2014. *Defying Convention: US Resistance to the UN Treaty on Women's Rights.* New York: Cambridge University Press.

Banaji, Mahzarin R., and Anthony G. Greenwald. 2016. *Blindspot: Hidden Biases of Good People.* New York: Bantam.

Barnes, Tiffany D., and Emily Beaulieu. 2014. "Gender Stereotypes and Corruption: How Candidates Affect Perceptions of Election Fraud." *Politics & Gender* 10.3: 365–391.

Baum, Michael, and Ana Espírito-Santo. 2012. "Portugal's Quota-Parity Law: An Analysis of Its Adoption." *West European Politics* 35.2: 319–342.

Beckwith, Karen. 2000. "Beyond Compare? Women's Movements in Comparative Perspective." *European Journal of Political Research* 37.4: 431–468.

Beckwith, Karen. 2003. "The Gendering Ways of States: Women's Representation and State Recognition in France, Great Britain, and the United States." In *Women's Movements Facing the Reconfigured State*, eds. Lee Ann Banaszak, Karen Beckwith, and Dieter Rucht. New York: Cambridge University Press.

Beckwith, Karen. 2013. "The Comparative Study of Women's Movements." In *The Oxford Handbook of Gender and Politics*, eds. Georgina Waylen, Karen Celis, Johanna Kantola, and S. Laurel Weldon. New York: Oxford University Press.

Bell, Andrew, and Kelvyn Jones. 2015. "Explaining Fixed Effects: Random Effects Modeling of Time-Series, Cross-Sectional, and Panel Data." *Political Science Research and Methods* 3.1: 133–153.

Bem, Sandra Lipsitz. 1981."Gender Schema Theory: A Cognitive Account of Sex Typing." *Psychological Review* 88.4: 354–364.

Berdahl, Jennifer L. 2007. "Harassment Based on Sex: Protecting Social Status in the Context of Gender Hierarchy." *Academy of Management Review* 32.2: 641–658.

Bettencourt, B., and Bruce D. Bartholow. 1998. "The Importance of Status Legitimacy for Intergroup Attitudes among Numerical Minorities." *Journal of Social Issues* 54.4: 759–775.

Bjarnegård, Elin. 2013. *Gender, Informal Institutions, and Political Recruitment: Explaining Male Dominance in Parliamentary Representation*. New York: Palgrave Macmillan.

Bonder, Gloria, and Marcela Nari. 1995. "The 30 Percent Quota Law: A Turning Point for Women's Political Participation in Argentina." In *A Rising Public Voice: Women in Politics Worldwide*, ed. Alida Brill. New York: The Feminist Press at the City University of New York Press.

Brown, Elizabeth R., Amanda B. Diekman, and Monica C. Schneider. 2011. "A Change Will Do Us Good: Threats Diminish Typical Preferences for Male Leaders." *Personality and Social Psychology Bulletin* 37.7: 930–941.

Bruhn, Kathleen. 2003. "Whores and Lesbians: Political Activism, Party Strategies, and Gender Quotas in Mexico." *Electoral Studies* 22.1: 101–119.

Burrell, Barbara. 1994. *A Woman's Place Is in the House*. Ann Arbor: University of Michigan Press.

Bush, Sarah Sunn. 2011. "International Politics and the Spread of Quotas for Women in Legislatures." *International Organization* 65.1: 103–137.

Bush, Sarah Sunn. 2015. *The Taming of Democracy Assistance*. New York: Cambridge University Press.

Bush, Sarah Sunn, and Eleanor Gao. 2017. "Small Tribes, Big Gains: The Strategic Uses of Gender Quotas in the Middle East." *Comparative Politics* 49.2: 149–167.

Cain, Bruce, John Ferejohn, and Morris Fiorina. 1987. *The Personal Vote: Constituency Service and Electoral Independence*. Cambridge: Harvard University Press.

Carey, John M., and Matthew Shugart. 1995. "Incentives to Cultivate a Personal Vote: A Rank Ordering of Electoral Formulas." *Electoral Studies* 14.4: 417–439.

Carothers, Thomas. 2016. *Democracy Support Strategies: Leading with Women's Political Empowerment*. Washington, DC: Carnegie Endowment for International Peace.

Caul, Miki. 1999. "Women's Representation in Parliament: The Role of Political Parties." *Party Politics* 5.1: 79–98.

Caul, Miki. 2001. "Political Parties and the Adoption of Candidate Gender Quotas: A Cross-National Analysis." *Journal of Politics* 63.4: 1214–1229.

Chama, Mónica. 2001. *Las Mujeres y el Poder*. Buenos Aires: Ciudad Argentina.

Charrad, Mounira M. 2011. "Gender in the Middle East: Islam, State, Agency." *Annual Review of Sociology* 37: 417–437.

Cheng, Christine, and Margit Tavits. 2011. "Informal Influences in Selecting Female Political Candidates." *Political Research Quarterly* 64.2: 460–471.

Chowdhury, Farah Deeba. 2009. "Problems of Women's Participation in Bangladesh Politics." *The Round Table* 98.404: 555–567.

Clayton, Amanda, Diana Z. O'Brien, and Jennifer M. Piscopo. 2018. "All Male Panels? Representation and Democratic Legitimacy." *American Journal of Political Science*. https://onlinelibrary.wiley.com/doi/full/10.1111/ajps.12391 (October 14, 2018).

Closa, Carlos, and Paul Heywood. 2004. *Spain and the European Union*. New York: Palgrave Macmillan.

Clucas, Richard, and Melody Ellis Valdini. 2015. *The Character of Democracy: How Institutions Shape Politics*. New York: Oxford University Press.

Coakley, John. 2003. "The Election and Party System." In *How Ireland Voted 2002*, eds. Michael Gallagher, Michael Marsh, and Paul Mitchell. London: Palgrave Macmillan.

Collins, Stephen. 2003. "Campaign Strategies." In *How Ireland Voted 2002*, eds. Michael Gallagher, Michael Marsh, and Paul Mitchell. London: Palgrave Macmillan.

Connolly, Linda. 2002. *The Irish Women's Movement*. London: Palgrave Macmillan.

Cook, Linda J., and Carol Nechemias. 2009. "Women in the Russian State Duma." In *Women in Power in Post-Communist Parliament*, eds. Marilyn Rueschemeyer and Sharon L. Wolchik. Bloomington: Indiana University Press.

Coppedge, Michael, et al. 2011. "Conceptualizing and Measuring Democracy: A New Approach." *Perspectives on Politics* 9.2: 247–267.

Corrales, Javier. 2000. "Presidents, Ruling Parties, and Party Rules: A Theory on the Politics of Economic Reform in Latin America." *Comparative Politics* 32.2: 127–149.

Dahlerup, Drude, and Lenita Freidenvall. 2005. "Quotas as a 'Fast Track' to Equal Representation for Women: Why Scandinavia Is No Longer the Model." *International Feminist Journal of Politics* 7.1: 26–48.

Darcy, Robert, Susan Welch, and Janet Clark. 1994. *Women, Elections, and Representation*. Lincoln: University of Nebraska Press.

Davidson-Schmich, Louise K. 2006. "Implementation of Political Party Gender Quotas: Evidence from the German Länder 1990–2000." *Party Politics* 12.2: 211–232.

Derks, Belle, Colette Van Laar, and Naomi Ellemers. 2016. "The Queen Bee Phenomenon: Why Women Leaders Distance Themselves from Junior Women." *The Leadership Quarterly* 27.3: 456–469.

Diamond, Larry. 2002. "Thinking about Hybrid Regimes." *Journal of Democracy* 13.2: 21–35.

Dolan, Kathleen. 2010. "The Impact of Gender Stereotyped Evaluations on Support for Women Candidates." *Political Behavior* 32.1: 69–88.

Downs, Anthony. 1957. "An Economic Theory of Political Action in a Democracy." *Journal of Political Economy* 65.2: 135–150.

Druckman, James N., and Cindy D. Kam. 2011. "Students as Experimental Participants." In *Cambridge Handbook of Experimental Political Science*, eds. James N. Druckman et al. New York: Cambridge University Press.

Dubrow, Joshua Kjerulf. 2011. "The Importance of Party Ideology: Explaining Parliamentarian Support for Political Party Gender Quotas in Eastern Europe." *Party Politics* 17.5: 561–579.

Eagly, Alice H., and Linda Lorene Carli. 2007. *Through the Labyrinth: The Truth about How Women Become Leaders*. Boston: Harvard Business Press.

Eagly, Alice H., and Steven J. Karau. 2002. "Role Congruity Theory of Prejudice toward Female Leaders." *Psychological Review* 109.3: 573–598.

Eagly, Alice H., and Antonio Mladinic. 1994. "Are People Prejudiced against Women? Some Answers from Research on Attitudes, Gender Stereotypes, and Judgments of Competence." *European Review of Social Psychology* 5.1: 1–35.

Ellemers, Naomi, et al. 2012. "Women in High Places: When and Why Promoting Women into Top Positions Can Harm Them Individually or as a Group (and How to Prevent This)." *Research in Organizational Behavior* 32: 163–187.

Esarey, Justin, and Leslie Schwindt-Bayer. 2017. "Estimating Causal Relationships between Women's Representation in Government and Corruption." http://www.justinesarey.com/gender-corruption-and-causality.pdf (October 13, 2018).

Espírito-Santo, Ana, and Edalina Rodrigues Sanches. 2018. "Looking for Locals Under a Closed-List Proportional Representation System: The Case of Portugal." *Electoral Studies* 52: 117–127.

Falk, Erika, and Kate Kenski. 2006. "Issue Saliency and Gender Stereotypes: Support for Women as Presidents in Times of War and Terrorism." *Social Science Quarterly* 87.1: 1–18.

Faludi, Susan. 1991. *Backlash: The Undeclared War against Women*. London: Vintage.

Fenno, Richard Francis. 1978. *Home Style: House Members in Their Districts*. New Yorks: Harper Collins.

Ferber, Marianne A., and Phyllis Hutton Raabe. 2003. "Women in the Czech Republic: Feminism, Czech Style." *International Journal of Politics, Culture, and Society* 16.3: 407–430.

Ferreira, Virgínia. 2011. "Engendering Portugal: Social Change, State Politics, and Women's Social Mobilization." In *Contemporary Portugal: Politics, Society and Culture*, ed. António Costa Pinto. New York: Columbia University Press.

Franceschet, Susan. 2010. "Explaining Domestic Violence Policy Outcomes in Chile and Argentina." *Latin American Politics and Society* 52.3: 1–29.

Franceschet, Susan, and Jennifer M. Piscopo. 2008. "Gender Quotas and Women's Substantive Representation: Lessons from Argentina." *Politics & Gender* 4.3: 393–425.

Fraser, Nicholas, and Marysa Navarro. 1996. *Evita*. New York: W. W. Norton & Company.

Freedom House. 2004. "Bangladesh." *Freedom in the World 2004.* https://freedomhouse.org/report/freedom-world/2004/bangladesh (October 15, 2018).

Freire, André, and José Manuel Leite Viegas. 2009. "Inquérito à População Portuguesa: Base de Dados, 2008." In *Representação Política em Portugal: Inqéritos e Bases de Dados*, eds. André Freire, José Manuel Leite Viegas, and Filipa Seiceira. Lisbon: ICS.

Gallagher, Michael, and Michael Marsh. 1988. *Candidate Selection in Comparative Perspective: The Secret Garden on Politics.* Newbury Park, CA: Sage Publications.

Galligan, Yvonne. 2003. "Candidate Selection: More Democratic or More Centrally Controlled?" In *How Ireland Voted 2002*, eds. Michael Gallagher, Michael Marsh, and Paul Mitchell. London: Palgrave Macmillan.

Garcia-Retamero, Rocio, and Esther López-Zafra. 2006. "Prejudice against Women in Male-Congenial Environments: Perceptions of Gender Role Congruity in Leadership." *Sex Roles* 55.1-2: 51–61.

Gelman, Andrew, and Gary King. 1990. "Estimating Incumbency Advantage without Bias." *American Journal of Political Science* 34.4: 1142–1164.

Gerlach, Christian. 2010. *Extremely Violent Societies: Mass Violence in the Twentieth-Century World.* New York: Cambridge University Press.

Giannetti, Daniela, Bernard Grofman, and Steven R. Reed. 2014. "Studying Electoral Engineering via a Double Barrelled Natural Experiment: Comparing the Long-Run Consequences of 1990s Electoral Reform in Italy and Japan." In *Italy and Japan: How Similar Are They? A Comparative Analysis of Politics, Economics, and International Relations*, eds. Silvio Beretta, Axel Berkofsky, and Fabio Rugge. Milano: Springer.

Glick, Peter, et al. 2000. "Beyond Prejudice as Simple Antipathy: Hostile and Benevolent Sexism across Cultures." *Journal of Personality and Social Psychology* 79.5: 763.

Glick, Peter, and Susan T. Fiske. 1996. "The Ambivalent Sexism Inventory: Differentiating Hostile and Benevolent Sexism." *Journal of Personality and Social Psychology* 70.3: 491.

Goetz, Anne Marie. 2003. "Women's Political Effectiveness: A Conceptual Framework." In *No Shortcuts to Power: African Women in Politics and Policy Making*, eds. Anne Marie Goetz and Shireen Hassim. Chicago: University of Chicago Press.

Goetz, Anne Marie. 2007. "Political Cleaners: Women as the New Anti-Corruption Force?" *Development and Change* 38.1: 87–105.

Golden, Miriam A., and Lucio Picci. 2005. "Proposal for a New Measure of Corruption, Illustrated with Italian Data." *Economics & Politics* 17.1: 37–75.

Goulart, Pedro, and Francisco José Veiga. 2016. "Portuguese 2015 Legislative Elections: How Economic Voting, the Median Voter, and Unemployment Led to 'The Times they are a'Changin.'" *Electoral Studies* 43: 197–200.

Greenwald, Anthony G., and Linda Hamilton Krieger. 2006. "Implicit Bias: Scientific Foundations." *California Law Review* 94.4: 945–967.

Guadagnini, Marila. 2005. "Gendering the Debate on Political Representation in Italy: A Difficult Challenge." In *State Feminism and Political Representation*, eds. Joni Lovenduski and Claudie Baudino. New York: Cambridge University Press.

Gudina, Merera. 2011. "Elections and Democratization in Ethiopia, 1991–2010." *Journal of Eastern African Studies* 5.4: 664–680.

Hagmann, Tobias, and Jon Abbink. 2011. "Twenty Years of Revolutionary Democratic Ethiopia, 1991 to 2012." *Journal of Eastern African Studies* 5.4: 579–595.

Halder, Nomita. 2004. "Female Representation in Parliament: A Case Study from Bangladesh." *New Zealand Journal of Asian Studies* 6.1: 27–63.

Hazan, Reuven Y., and Gideon Rahat. 2010. *Democracy within Parties: Candidate Selection Methods and Their Political Consequences*. New York: Oxford University Press.

Heilman, Madeline E., and Tyler G. Okimoto. 2007. "Why Are Women Penalized for Success at Male Tasks? The Implied Communality Deficit." *Journal of Applied Psychology* 92.1: 81–92.

Hinojosa, Magda. 2012. *Selecting Women, Electing Women: Political Representation and Candidate Selection in Latin America*. Philadelphia: Temple University Press.

Holman, Mirya R., Jennifer L. Merolla, and Elizabeth J. Zechmeister. 2011. "Sex, Stereotypes, and Security: A Study of the Effects of Terrorist Threat on Assessments of Female Leadership." *Journal of Women, Politics & Policy* 32.3: 173–192.

Holman, Mirya R., Jennifer L. Merolla, and Elizabeth J. Zechmeister. 2016. "Terrorist Threat, Male Stereotypes, and Candidate Evaluations." *Political Research Quarterly* 69.1: 134–147.

Holman, Otto. 1996. *Integrating Southern Europe: EC Expansion and the Transnationalization of Spain*. New York: Routledge.

Htun, Mala. 2004. "Is Gender Like Ethnicity? The Political Representation of Identity Groups." *Perspectives on Politics* 2.3: 439–458.

Htun, Mala N., and Mark P. Jones. 2002. "Engendering the Right to Participate in Decision-Making: Electoral Quotas and Women's Leadership in Latin America." In *Gender and the Politics of Rights and Democracy in Latin America*, eds. Nikki Craske and Maxine Molyneux. New York: Palgrave Macmillan.

Htun, Mala, Marina Lacalle, and Juan Pablo Micozzi. 2013. "Does Women's Presence Change Legislative Behavior? Evidence from Argentina, 1983–2007." *Journal of Politics in Latin America* 5.1: 95–125.

Huddy, Leonie, and Theresa Capelos. 2002. "Gender Stereotyping and Candidate Evaluation." In *The Social Psychology of Politics*, eds. Victor C Ottati et al. New York: Springer.

Huddy, Leonie, and Nayda Terkildsen. 1993. "Gender Stereotypes and the Perception of Male and Female Candidates." *American Journal of Political Science* 37.1: 119–147.

Hughes, Melanie M. 2008. "Politics at the Intersection: A Cross-National Analysis of Minority Women's Legislative Representation." Diss. Ohio State University.

Hughes, Melanie M. 2009. "Armed Conflict, International Linkages, and Women's Parliamentary Representation in Developing Nations." *Social Problems* 56.1: 174–204.

Hughes, Melanie M., and Aili Mari Tripp. 2015. "Civil War and Trajectories of Change in Women's Political Representation in Africa, 1985–2010." *Social Forces* 93.4: 1513–1540.

Inglehart, Ronald, and Pippa Norris. 2003. *Rising Tide: Gender Equality and Cultural Change Around the World*. New York: Cambridge University Press.

IPU (Inter-Parliamentary Union). 2011. "Women in Parliament in 2011: The Year in Perspective." www.ipu.org/pdf/publications/wmnpersp11-e.pdf (October 15, 2018).

Isaacs-Martin, Wendy. 2016. "Political and Ethnic Identity in Violent Conflict: The Case of Central African Republic." *International Journal of Conflict and Violence* 10.1: 26–39.

Iyengar, Shanto, and Donald R. Kinder. 1987. *News that Matters: Agenda-Setting and Priming in a Television Age.* Chicago: University of Chicago Press.

Jones, Mark P. 1998. "Gender Quotas, Electoral Laws, and the Election of Women: Lessons from the Argentine Provinces." *Comparative Political Studies* 31.1: 3–21.

Jones, Mark P. 2009. "Gender Quotas, Electoral Laws, and the Election of Women: Evidence from the Latin American Vanguard." *Comparative Political Studies* 42.1: 56–81.

Kahn, Kim Fridkin. 1994. "The Distorted Mirror: Press Coverage of Women Candidates for Statewide Office." *The Journal of Politics* 56.1: 154–173.

Kahneman, Daniel, Paul Slovic, and Amos Tversky. 1982. *Judgment Under Uncertainty.* New York: Cambridge University Press.

Kang, Alice J., and Aili Mari Tripp. 2018. "Coalitions Matter: Citizenship, Women, and Quota Adoption in Africa." *Perspectives on Politics* 16.1: 73–91.

Khan, Adeeba Aziz. 2015. "The Politics of Constitutional Amendments in Bangladesh: The Case of the Non-Political Caretaker Government." *International Review of Law* 9.

Khan, Salma, Mahmuda Islam, and Jahanara Huq, eds. 2005. "The Advancement of Women in Bangladesh: Gaps and Challenges." Dhaka: NGO Coalition on Beijing Process (NCBP).

King, Elizabeth, and Andrew Mason. 2001. "Engendering Development: Through Gender Equality in Rights, Resources, and Voice." World Bank Policy Reasearch Report 21776. World Bank and Oxford University Press. http://documents.worldbank.org/curated/en/512911468327401785/Engendering-development-through-gender-equality-in-rights-resources-and-voice (October 14, 2018).

Kitschelt, Herbert. 2013. "Dataset of the Democratic Accountability and Linkages Project (DALP)." Duke University.

Klašnja, Marko. 2015. "Corruption and the Incumbency Disadvantage: Theory and Evidence." *The Journal of Politics* 77.4: 928–942.

Koenig, Anne M., Alice H. Eagly, Abigail A. Mitchell, and Tiina Ristikari. 2011. "Are Leader Stereotypes Masculine? A Meta-Analysis of Three Research Paradigms." *Psychological Bulletin* 137.4: 616–642.

Krook, Mona Lena. 2007. "Candidate Gender Quotas: A Framework for Analysis." *European Journal of Political Research* 46.3: 367–394.

Krook, Mona Lena. 2009. *Quotas for Women in Politics: Gender and Candidate Selection Reform Worldwide.* New York: Oxford University Press.

Krook, Mona Lena. 2016. "Contesting Gender Quotas: Dynamics of Resistance." *Politics, Groups, and Identities* 4.2: 268–283.

Krook, Mona Lena. 2017. "Violence Against Women in Politics." *Journal of Democracy* 28.1: 74–88.

Krosnick, Jon A., and Donald R. Kinder. 1990. "Altering the Foundations of Support for the President through Priming." *American Political Science Review* 84.2: 497–512.

Krupnikov, Yanna, Spencer Piston, and Nichole M. Bauer. 2016. "Saving Face: Identifying Voter Responses to Black Candidates and Female Candidates." *Political Psychology* 37.2: 253–273.

Kunovich, Sheri, and Pamela Paxton. 2005. "Pathways to Power: The Role of Political Parties in Women's National Political Representation." *American Journal of Sociology* 111.2: 505–552.

Lawless, Jennifer L. 2004. "Women, War, and Winning Elections: Gender Stereotyping in the Post-September 11th Era." *Political Research Quarterly* 57.3: 479–490.

Lawless, Jennifer L., and Richard L. Fox. 2005. *It Takes a Candidate: Why Women Don't Run for Office.* New York: Cambridge University Press.

Lawless, Jennifer L., and Richard L. Fox. 2010. *It Still Takes a Candidate: Why Women Don't Run for Office.* New York: Cambridge University Press.

Leijenaar, Monique. 1993. "A Battle for Power: Selecting Candidates in the Netherlands." In *Gender and Party Politics*, eds. Pippa Norris and Joni Lovenduski. London: Sage.

Levi, Margaret. 1997. "A Model, a Method, and a Map: Rational Choice in Comparative and Historical Analysis." In *Comparative Politics: Rationality, Culture, and Structure*, eds. Mark Irving Lichbach and Alan S. Zuckerman. New York: Cambridge University Press.

Levi, Margaret, Audrey Sacks, and Tom Tyler. 2009. "Conceptualizing Legitimacy, Measuring Legitimating Beliefs." *American Behavioral Scientist* 53.3: 354–375.

Lisi, Marco. 2015. *Party Change, Recent Democracies, and Portugal: Comparative Perspectives.* London: Lexington Books.

López-Sáez, Mercedes, J. Francisco Morales, and Ana Lisbona. 2008. "Evolution of Gender Stereotypes in Spain: Traits and Roles." *The Spanish Journal of Psychology* 11.2: 609–617.

Lopez-Zafra, Esther, and Rocio Garcia-Retamero. 2012. "Do Gender Stereotypes Change? The Dynamic of Gender Stereotypes in Spain." *Journal of Gender Studies* 21.2: 169–183.

Lundell, Krister. 2004. "Determinants of Candidate Selection: The Degree of Centralization in Comparative Perspective." *Party Politics* 10.1: 25–47.

Matland, Richard E. 1993. "Institutional Variables Affecting Female Representation in National Legislatures: The Case of Norway." *The Journal of Politics* 55.3: 737–755.

Matland, Richard E. 1998. "Women's Representation in National Legislatures: Developed and Developing Countries." *Legislative Studies Quarterly* 23.1: 109–125.

Matland, Richard E. 2005. "Enhancing Women's Political Participation: Legislative Recruitment and Electoral Systems." In *Women in Parliament: Beyond Numbers*, eds. Julie Ballington and Azza Karam. Stockholm: International IDEA.

Matland, Richard E., and Deborah Dwight Brown. 1992. "District Magnitude's Effect on Female Representation in US State Legislatures." *Legislative Studies Quarterly* 17.4: 469–492.

Matland, Richard E., and Kathleen A. Montgomery. 2003. "Recruiting Women to National Legislatures: A General Framework with Applications to Post-Communist Democracies." In *Women's Access to Political Power in Post-Communist Europe*, eds. Richard E. Matland and Kathleen A. Montgomery. New York: Oxford University Press.

Matland, Richard E., and Donley T. Studlar. 1996. "The Contagion of Women Candidates in Single-Member District and Proportional Representation Electoral Systems: Canada and Norway." *The Journal of Politics* 58.3: 707–733.

McCammon, Holly J., Karen E. Campbell, Ellen M. Granberg, and Christine Mowery. 2001. "How Movements Win: Gendered Opportunity Structures and US Women's Suffrage Movements, 1866 to 1919." *American Sociological Review* 66.1: 49–70.

McDermott, Monika L. 1998. "Race and Gender Cues in Low-Information Elections." *Political Research Quarterly* 51.4: 895–918.

McElroy, Gail, and Michael Marsh. 2010. "Candidate Gender and Voter Choice: Analysis from a Multimember Preferential Voting System." *Political Research Quarterly* 63.4: 822–833.

McElroy, Gail, and Michael Marsh. 2011. "Electing Women to the Dáil: Gender Cues and the Irish Voter." *Irish Political Studies* 26.4: 521–534.

McGing, Claire. 2013. "The Single Transferable Vote and Women's Representation in Ireland." *Irish Political Studies* 28.3: 322–340.

McGuire, James. 1995. "Political Parties and Democracy in Argentina." In *Building Democratic Institutions: Party Systems in Latin America*, eds. Scott Mainwaring and Timothy R. Scully. Stanford: Stanford University Press.

Melo, Daniela. 2017. "Women's Movements in Portugal and Spain: Democratic Processes and Policy Outcomes." *Journal of Women, Politics & Policy* 38.3: 251–275.

Milkias, Paulos. 2011. *Ethiopia*. Santa Barbara, CA: ABC-CLIO.

Moghadam, Valentine M. 2003. *Modernizing Women: Gender and Social Change in the Middle East*. London: Lynne Rienner Publishers.

Moniruzzaman, Mohammed. 2009. "Parliamentary Democracy in Bangladesh: An Evaluation of the Parliament During 1991–2006." *Commonwealth & Comparative Politics* 47.1: 100–126.

Montabes, Juan, and Carmen Ortega. 1999. "Candidate Selection in Two Rigid List Systems: Spain and Portugal." Paper Presented at the ECPR Joint Workshops in Mannheim, March 26–31.

Monteiro, Rosa, and Virgínia Ferreira. 2016. "Women's Movements and the State in Portugal: A State Feminism Approach." *Sociedade e Estado* 31.2: 459–486.

Murphy, Gary. 2003. "The Background to the Election." In *How Ireland Voted 2002*, eds. Michael Gallagher, Michael Marsh, and Paul Mitchell. London: Palgrave Macmillan.

Murray, Rainbow. 2004. "Why Didn't Parity Work? A Closer Examination of the 2002 Election Results." *French Politics* 2.3: 347–362.

Murray, Rainbow. 2010. *Parties, Gender Quotas and Candidate Selection in France*. Basingstoke: Palgrave Macmillan.

Murray, Rainbow, Mona Lena Krook, and Katherine A.R. Opello. 2012. "Why Are Gender Quotas Adopted? Party Pragmatism and Parity in France." *Political Research Quarterly* 65.3: 529–543.

Müller, Wolfgang C., and Kaare Strøm, eds. 1999. *Policy, Office, or Votes? How Political Parties in Western Europe Make Hard Decisions*. New York: Cambridge University Press.

Norris, Pippa. 1985. "Women's Legislative Participation in Western Europe." *West European Politics* 8.4: 90–101.

Norris, Pippa, ed. 1997. *Passages to Power: Legislative Recruitment in Advanced Democracies*. New York: Cambridge University Press.

Norris, Pippa. 2004. *Electoral Engineering: Voting Rules and Political Behavior*. New York: Cambridge University Press.

Norris, Pippa, and Ronald Inglehart. 2001. "Cultural Obstacles to Equal Representation." *Journal of Democracy* 12.3: 126–140.

Norris, Pippa, and Joni Lovenduski. 1993. "'If Only More Candidates Came Forward': Supply-Side Explanations of Candidate Selection in Britain." *British Journal of Political Science* 23.3: 373–408.

Norris, Pippa, and Joni Lovenduski. 1995. *Political Recruitment: Gender, Race and Class in the British Parliament*. New York: Cambridge University Press.

O'Brien, Diana Z. 2015. "Rising to the Top: Gender, Political Performance, and Party Leadership in Parliamentary Democracies." *American Journal of Political Science* 59.4: 1022–1039.

O'Connor, Pat. 2008. "The Irish Patriarchal State: Continuity and Change." In *Contesting the State: Lessons from the Irish Case*, eds. Maura Adshead, Peadar Kirby, and Michelle Millar. Manchester, UK: Manchester University Press.

Osman, Ferdous Arfina. 2010. "Bangladesh Politics: Confrontation, Monopoly, and Crisis in Governance." *Asian Journal of Political Science* 18.3: 310–333.

Paasilinna, Silja. 2016. *Women's Reserved Seats in Bangladesh: A Systemic Analysis of Meaningful Representation*. Arlington, VA: International Foundation for Electoral Systems.

Palici di Suni, Elisabetta. 2012. "Gender Parity and Quotas in Italy: A Convoluted Reform Process." *West European Politics* 35.2: 380–394.

Panday, Pranab Kumar. 2008. "Representation without Participation: Quotas for Women in Bangladesh." *International Political Science Review* 29.4: 489–512.

Paxton, Pamela, and Melanie M. Hughes. 2015. "The Increasing Effectiveness of National Gender Quotas, 1990–2010." *Legislative Studies Quarterly* 40.3: 331–362.

Paxton, Pamela, and Melanie M. Hughes. 2017. *Women, Politics, and Power: A Global Perspective*. 3rd ed. Thousand Oaks, CA: CQ Press.

Paxton, Pamela, and Sheri Kunovich. 2003. "Women's Political Representation: The Importance of Ideology." *Social Forces* 82.1: 87–113.

Phillips, Anne. 1995. *The Politics of Presence*. New York: Oxford University Press.

Piscopo, Jennifer. 2019. "The Limits of Leaning In: Ambition, Recruitment, and Candidate Training in Comparative Perspective." *Politics, Groups, and Identities*. In Press.

Riaz, Ali. 2005. "Bangladesh in 2004: The Politics of Vengeance and the Erosion of Democracy." *Asian Survey* 45.1: 112–118.

Riedl, Rachel Beatty, and J. Tyler Dickovick. 2014. "Party Systems and Decentralization in Africa." *Studies in Comparative International Development* 49.3: 321–342.

Rosenbluth, Frances, Rob Salmond, and Michael F. Thies. 2006. "Welfare Works: Explaining Female Legislative Representation." *Politics & Gender* 2.2: 165–192.

Ruble, Diane N., Leah E. Lurye, and Kristina M. Zosuls. 2007. "Pink Frilly Dresses (PFD) and Early Gender Identity." *Princeton Report on Knowledge* 2.2.

Rudman, Laurie A. 1998. "Self-Promotion as a Risk Factor for Women: The Costs and Benefits of Counterstereotypical Impression Management." *Journal of Personality and Social Psychology* 74.3: 629–645.

Rudman, Laurie A., et al. 2012. "Status Incongruity and Backlash Effects: Defending the Gender Hierarchy Motivates Prejudice against Female Leaders." *Journal of Experimental Social Psychology* 48.1: 165–179.

Rudman, Laurie A., and Peter Glick. 2001. "Prescriptive Gender Stereotypes and Backlash toward Agentic Women." *Journal of Social Issues* 57.4: 743–762.

Rudman, Laurie A., Anthony G. Greenwald, and Debbie E. McGhee. 2001. "Implicit Self-Concept and Evaluative Implicit Gender Stereotypes: Self and Ingroup Share Desirable Traits." *Personality and Social Psychology Bulletin* 27.9: 1164–1178.

Rule, Wilma. 1981. "Why Women Don't Run: The Critical Contextual Factors in Women's Legislative Recruitment." *Western Political Quarterly* 34.1: 60–77.

Rule, Wilma. 1987. "Electoral Systems, Contextual Factors, and Women's Opportunity for Election to Parliament in Twenty-Three Democracies." *Western Political Quarterly* 40.3: 477–498.

Ryan, Michelle K., et al. 2016. "Getting on Top of the Glass Cliff: Reviewing a Decade of Evidence, Explanations, and Impact." *The Leadership Quarterly* 27.3: 446–455.

Ryan, Michelle K., and S. Alexander Haslam. 2005. "The Glass Cliff: Evidence That Women Are Over-Represented in Precarious Leadership Positions." *British Journal of Management* 16.2: 81–90.

Ryan, Michelle K., and S. Alexander Haslam. 2007. "The Glass Cliff: Exploring the Dynamics Surrounding the Appointment of Women to Precarious Leadership Positions." *Academy of Management Review* 32.2: 549–572.

Ryan, Michelle K., S. Alexander Haslam, and Clara Kulich. 2010. "Politics and the Glass Cliff: Evidence That Women Are Preferentially Selected to Contest Hard-to-Win Seats." *Psychology of Women Quarterly* 34.1: 56–64.

Saint-Germain, Michelle A. 1993. "Women in Power in Nicaragua: Myth and Reality." In *Women as National Leaders*, ed. M. A. Genovese. Newbury Park, CA: Sage.

Salmenniemi, Suvi, and Maria Adamson. 2015. "New Heroines of Labour: Domesticating Post-Feminism and Neoliberal Capitalism in Russia." *Sociology* 49.1: 88–105.

Sanbonmatsu, Kira. 2002. "Gender Stereotypes and Vote Choice." *American Journal of Political Science* 46.1: 20–34.

Schein, Virginia E. 1975. "Relationships between Sex Role Stereotypes and Requisite Management Characteristics among Female Managers." *Journal of Applied Psychology* 60.3: 340–344.

Schmidt, Gregory D. 2003. "Unanticipated Successes: Lessons from Peru's Experiences with Gender Quotas in Majoritarian Closed List and Open List PR Systems." Paper Presented at the International IDEA Workshop, Lima, Peru.

Schwindt-Bayer, Leslie A. 2005. "The Incumbency Disadvantage and Women's Election to Legislative Office." *Electoral Studies* 24.2: 227–244.

Schwindt-Bayer, Leslie A. 2009. "Making Quotas Work: The Effect of Gender Quota Laws on the Election of Women." *Legislative Studies Quarterly* 34.1: 5–28.

Schwindt-Bayer, Leslie A. 2010. *Political Power and Women's Representation in Latin America*. New York: Oxford University Press.

Schwindt-Bayer, Leslie A., and Santiago Alles. 2018. "Women in Legislatures: Gender, Institutions, and Democracy." In *Gender and Representation in Latin America*, ed. Leslie A. Schwindt-Bayer. New York: Oxford University Press.

Schwindt-Bayer, Leslie A., Michael Malecki, and Brian F. Crisp. 2010. "Candidate Gender and Electoral Success in Single Transferable Vote Systems." *British Journal of Political Science* 40.3: 693–709.

Sczesny, Sabine, et al. 2004. "Gender Stereotypes and the Attribution of Leadership Traits: A Cross-Cultural Comparison." *Sex Roles* 51.11: 631–645.

Seligson, Mitchell A. 2002. "The Impact of Corruption on Regime Legitimacy: A Comparative Study of Four Latin American Countries." *The Journal of Politics* 64.2: 408–433.

Serbin, Lisa A., et al. 2001. "Gender Stereotyping in Infancy: Visual Preferences for and Knowledge of Gender-Stereotyped Toys in the Second Year." *International Journal of Behavioral Development* 25.1: 7–15.

Shames, Shauna. 2003. "The 'Un-Candidates': Gender and Outsider Signals in Women's Political Advertisements." *Women & Politics* 25.1-2: 115–147.

Shugart, Mathew Søberg. 1994. "Minorities Represented and Unrepresented." In *Electoral Systems in Comparative Perspective: Their Impact on Women and Minorities*, eds. Wilma Rule and Joseph F. Zimmerman. London: Greenwood Press.

Shugart, Matthew Søberg, Melody Ellis Valdini, and Kati Suominen. 2005. "Looking for Locals: Voter Information Demands and Personal Vote-Earning Attributes of Legislators Under Proportional Representation." *American Journal of Political Science* 49.2: 437–449.

Spence, Janet T., and Camille E. Buckner. 2000. "Instrumental and Expressive Traits, Trait Stereotypes, and Sexist Attitudes: What Do They Signify?" *Psychology of Women Quarterly* 24.1: 44–53.

Sperling, Valerie. 2015. *Sex, Politics, and Putin: Political Legitimacy in Russia*. New York: Oxford University Press.

Streb, Matthew J., et al. 2007. "Social Desirability Effects and Support for a Female American President." *Public Opinion Quarterly* 72.1: 76–89.

Stremlau, Nicole. 2013. "The Press and the Political Restructuring of Ethiopia." In *Reconfiguring Ethiopia: The Politics of Authoritarian Reform*, eds. Jon Abbink and Tobias Hagmann. London: Routledge.

Strøm, Kaare. 1990. "A Behavioral Theory of Competitive Political Parties." *American Journal of Political Science* 34.2: 565–598.

Swamy, Anand, et al. 2001. "Gender and Corruption." *Journal of Development Economics* 64.1: 25–55.

Takagi, Shinji, et al. 2004. "The IMF and Argentina, 1991-2001." Independent Evaluation Office of the IMF. Washington, DC: International Monetary Fund. https://www.imf.org/en/Publications/Independent-Evaluation-Office-Reports/Issues/2016/12/31/The-IMF-and-Argentina-1991-2001-17590 (October 14, 2018).

Thames, Frank C., and Margaret S. Williams. 2010. "Incentives for Personal Votes and Women's Representation in Legislatures." *Comparative Political Studies* 43.12: 1575–1600.

Threlfall, Monica. 2005. "Towards Parity Representation in Party Politics." In *Gendering Spanish Democracy*, eds. Monica Threlfall, Christine Cousins, and Celia Valiente Fernandez. New York: Routledge.

Threlfall, Monica. 2007. "Explaining Gender Parity Representation in Spain: The Internal Dynamics of Parties." *West European Politics* 30.5: 1068–1095.

Tremblay, Manon, and Réjean Pelletier. 2001. "More Women Constituency Party Presidents: A Strategy for Increasing the Number of Women Candidates in Canada?" *Party Politics* 7.2: 157–190.

Tripp, Aili Mari, and Alice Kang. 2008. "The Global Impact of Quotas: On the Fast Track to Increased Female Legislative Representation." *Comparative Political Studies* 41.3: 338–361.

Tronvoll, Kjetil. 2009. "Ambiguous Elections: The Influence of Non-Electoral Politics in Ethiopian Democratisation." *The Journal of Modern African Studies* 47.3: 449–474.

Tyler, Tom R. 2006. *Why People Obey the Law*. Princeton, NJ: Princeton University Press.

Van Biezen, Ingrid. 2003. *Political Parties in New Democracies: Party Organization in Southern and East-Central Europe*. New York: Palgrave Macmillan.

Van der Vleuten, Anna. 2007. *The Price of Gender Equality: Member States and Governance in the European Union*. Hampshire, UK: Ashgate.

Valdini, Melody Ellis. 2012. "A Deterrent to Diversity: The Conditional Effect of Electoral Rules on the Nomination of Women Candidates." *Electoral Studies* 31.4: 740–749.

Valdini, Melody Ellis. 2013. "Electoral Institutions and the Manifestation of Bias: The Effect of the Personal Vote on the Representation of Women." *Politics & Gender* 9.1: 76–92.

Verge, Tània. 2010. "Gendering Representation in Spain: Opportunities and Limits of Gender Quotas." *Journal of Women, Politics & Policy* 31.2: 166–190.

Verge, Tània. 2012. "Institutionalising Gender Equality in Spain: From Party Quotas to Electoral Gender Quotas." *West European Politics* 35.2: 395–414.

Verge, Tània, and Ana Espírito-Santo. 2016. "Interactions between Party and Legislative Quotas: Candidate Selection and Quota Compliance in Portugal and Spain." *Government and Opposition* 51.3: 416–439.

Vial, Andrea C., Jaime L. Napier, and Victoria L. Brescoll. 2016. "A Bed of Thorns: Female Leaders and the Self-Reinforcing Cycle of Illegitimacy." *The Leadership Quarterly* 27.3: 400–414.

Ware, Alan. 1996. *Political Parties and Party Systems*. Oxford: Oxford University Press.

Webb, Paul, and Sarah Childs. 2012. "Gender Politics and Conservatism: The View from the British Conservative Party Grassroots." *Government and Opposition* 47.1: 21–48.

Weber, Max. 1946. "Politics as a Vocation." In *From Max Weber: Essays in Sociology*, ed. Hans Gerth and C Wright Mills. New York: Oxford University Press: 77-128.

Weber, Max. 1968. *On Charisma and Institution Building*. Chicago: University of Chicago Press.

Weeks, Ana Catalano, and Lisa Baldez. 2015. "Quotas and Qualifications: The Impact of Gender Quota Laws on the Qualifications of Legislators in the Italian Parliament." *European Political Science Review* 7.1: 119–144.

Weeks, John. 2018. "The Contemporary Latin American Economies: Neoliberal Reconstruction." In *Capital, Power, and Inequality in Latin America*, ed. Sandor Halebsky. New York: Routledge.

Weingast, Barry R. 1997. "The Political Foundations of Democracy and the Rule of the Law." *American Political Science Review* 91.2: 245–263.

Williams, John E., and Deborah L. Best. 1990. *Measuring Sex Stereotypes: A Multination Study, Rev ed*. Thousand Oaks, CA: Sage.

Zosuls, Kristina M., et al. 2009. "The Acquisition of Gender Labels in Infancy: Implications for Gender-Typed Play." *Developmental Psychology* 45.3: 688–701.

For the benefit of digital users, indexed terms that span two pages (e.g., 52–53) may, on occasion, appear on only one of those pages.